COACHING

LIFE-CHANGING

small group

LEADERS

Also by Bill Donahue

Building a Church of Small Groups
(with Russ Robinson)

Leading Life-Changing Small Groups
(with the Willow Creek Small Groups Team)

Seven Deadly Sins of Small Group Ministry
(with Russ Robinson)

Walking the Small Group Tightrope
(with Russ Robinson)

A PRACTICAL GUIDE FOR THOSE WHO LEAD
AND SHEPHERD SMALL GROUP LEADERS

COACHING
LIFE-CHANGING
small group
LEADERS

BILL DONAHUE
GREG BOWMAN

ZONDERVAN™
GRAND RAPIDS, MICHIGAN 49530 USA

WILLOW
Willow Creek Resources

ZONDERVAN.COM/
AUTHORTRACKER

Coaching Life-Changing Small Group Leaders
Copyright © 2006 by Willow Creek Association

Requests for information should be addressed to:
Zondervan, *Grand Rapids, Michigan 49530*

Library of Congress Cataloging-in-Publication Data

Donahue, Bill.
    Coaching life-changing small group leaders : a practical guide for those who lead and shepherd small group leaders / Bill Donahue and Greg Bowman.
      p. cm.
    ISBN-13: 978-0-310-25179-8
    ISBN-10: 0-310-25179-6
    1. Christian leadership. 2. Small groups. 3. Church group work. 4. Personal coaching. I. Bowman, Greg. II. Title.
BV652.1.D66 2006
253'.7—dc22
                                       2005031941

Interior design by Mark Sheeres

Printed in the United States of America

06 07 08 09 10 11 12 • 10 9 8 7 6 5 4 3 2 1

Contents

115023

Part 5: A Coach's World

Part 6: Building a Coaching Structure

A Guide for Small Group Ministry Point Leaders

Introduction

We are so excited that you have chosen to use this resource. We have put a lot of time and energy into it, drawing from our experience with Willow Creek and hundreds of other churches. In addition, each of us has been a coach. We have lived in your shoes and continue today to train, develop, and encourage small group leaders.

Here is what lies ahead as you read through this guide. First, you will get a clear picture of what it means to be a shepherd of leaders. As you discover what it means to be a coach, you will see why you are so important to the disciple-making ministry of the local church. As people connect in small groups, experiencing community together, a small group leader feels the responsibility of leading a group well. It can be challenging and spiritually draining sometimes.

That's where you come in. As a support to leaders, you help them to function in life-giving ways with group members. Leaders learn that you are a prayer warrior, an encourager, a listener, and a resource for their ministry. Both directly and indirectly, you play a key role in the growth of each member of a small group in your care.

In this guide you will discover the Coach's Key Practices—the four essential functions that will characterize your ministry to leaders. We have worked hard to help you carry out those key practices in creative and effective ways.

Once you understand those key practices, you'll see that we have provided you with the Coach's Toolbox, a section filled with practical, useful tips and resources for meeting with leaders and encouraging their growth. This section of *Coaching Life-Changing Small Group Leaders* will get the most wear and tear. You will return to it many times for what you need to carry out your ministry to leaders.

Then you will find a section that helps you manage your life and ministry so that it is sustainable. The last thing a leader needs is a coach who is constantly depleted or burned out. Our hope is that you will design a coaching approach that uses your time well, maximizes the strengths of your leaders, and allows you to engage in the other responsibilities and opportunities of life without guilt or regret.

Finally, there is a section for those of you who lead the small group ministry in your church. Though coaches will find this material interesting and helpful, it is designed primarily for those who are building the overall small group ministry. It addresses the issues related to building a coaching structure and providing the resources and support that coaches need to be effective.

So dive in and be encouraged! We believe you will find what you need to coach others in a way that brings blessing to the church and fruit to your ministry.

God bless you and your efforts!

—Bill and Greg

Part One

A Vision for Coaching

What is coaching? Why is it so essential to have people in the church who are willing to guide and encourage leaders? What does it look like when someone takes on this role and invests in the life of a leader?

In order to become and build effective coaches in the church, first we need to embrace a vision for the practice of coaching. It is often a misunderstood role, mistaken by some to mean "boss" or "fault-finder." But that's not coaching, at least not when the spiritual growth of leaders and church members is at stake. It is different from mere oversight or supervision. Coaching is personal, developmental, and supportive. Coaches bring out the best in leaders. So let's take a few moments to get a clearer picture of what is means to coach leaders in the church.

The Call to Coaching

An Unlikely Coach

John Donahue, Bill's dad, was in his forties when he became the head swimming coach of George Washington High School in Philadelphia. For fifteen years, the teams he coached remained undefeated in league competition. Think about that for a moment—fifteen undefeated seasons in a row. Obviously he had everything needed to establish such a winning tradition: years of swimming experience on a nationally ranked college team, the fastest swimmers in the league, and the greatest training facilities in the city of Philadelphia. With all of that, one would expect him to win. Except he didn't have all of these advantages—actually, he had none of them.

John was an unlikely swimming coach, and Washington High was an unlikely place for a swimming dynasty to take root. The team practiced only three days a week at a rented facility, because that was all the school budget allowed. The swim team also had the same challenge every scholastic sports program faced—constant turnover. A successful tradition was hard to establish as experienced swimmers graduated and were replaced by a cohort of skinny, wide-eyed freshmen who thought the "backstroke" was a massage technique and the "butterfly" a transformed caterpillar.

New challengers also threatened the tradition of winning. The teams Washington defeated one year often hired new coaches the next, who were eager to make their mark. These former college swimmers came to coaching armed with the latest training techniques and filled with the energy Donahue had twenty years earlier. The competition had studied his poolside techniques and practice regimen for one purpose only—to be the first team to defeat Washington High School in a dual meet. But for fifteen years, no one ever did.

Standing 6' 2" and weighing 265 pounds, Donahue was hardly the prototype for a championship swimming coach. He was a heavyweight wrestler in college, and prior to that, he was in the US Navy, where he re-fitted airplane engines on the USS *Hornet*. Throughout his entire life, he never swam competitively. What generated this success in swimming and in other sports he coached? I believe there were several likely factors—factors that apply to sports, business, ministry, or any endeavor that requires the development and support of people.

> *Consistency*: I believe that consistent coaching ensured the same discipline, values, winning attitude, and solid work ethic throughout those fifteen years. Donahue developed a rapport with swimmers and an enduring reputation of almost legendary stature. Students called him John "the Duke" Donahue, after screen actor John "the Duke" Wayne. New swimmers on the team gazed at him with awe and respect (as one might do to Penn State football icon Joe Paterno, or former Indiana basketball legend Bobby Knight).

Love: Though he could be hard on swimmers in practice, demanding their best and pushing them to their limits, Donahue also had a tender side. The team knew from the stories that circulated around school that he would do anything for swimmers or their families in times of need.

There were the cold, rainy winter nights that the Duke took stranded swimmers home from practice. Or the times when a few dollars for lunch money helped a struggling student make it through the week. He balanced a tough, courageous personality with a tender, loving heart. I think that is why his swimmers were willing to work so hard for him. He loved them, and they knew it.

Courage: Years before working at Washington, Donahue coached at a troubled inner-city school in Philadelphia. A large, brawny student—known fondly as the "Caveman"—jumped the Duke one day in the lunchroom, knocking him to the ground. Unfortunately, this colossal tyrant had no idea that the guy he just attacked had recently completed four years in the navy during World War II, followed by three years of wrestling in the heavyweight class at Temple University. In a few moments, the Caveman was tied up in knots, a pain-filled pile of twisted limbs in the arms of the Duke.

Students would later speak of the incident with awe. When word of the event traveled to Donahue's new school, students asked, "So whatever happened to the Caveman?" The Duke calmly replied, "I put him back in his cave." Though he kidded about the incident, it took courage to walk into that school each day. Crime ridden and drug infested, it was truly a dangerous place, even for big guys like John Donahue.

Coaching was in John's blood; he was made for it. Though he appeared an unlikely swim coach at times, in reality he was exactly what a coach should be—consistent and disciplined, a lover of those he coached, and courageous enough to do what was right and stay the course in the face of overwhelming odds or intense opposition. Today, at over eighty years of age, he is living in a retirement community made up mostly of people who are over sixty years old, and he is still coaching people. (He taught a woman to swim for the first time in her life—in just three lessons!) He would never say that he was qualified to be a championship coach—just that he was called. And he took that calling and learned all he could to be the best coach in the city.

What will you do with the calling God has placed on you?

The Underwhelmed Need Not Apply

God doesn't usually call people to easy jobs. Try finding someone who ever felt competent for the service God demanded of him or her. Moses trembled, Mary was troubled, and Paul was terrified! Callings rattle cages and rock boats. Callings shatter illusions of complacency, comfort, and ease. They sometimes startle and confuse; they provoke and prod. God often calls the overwhelmed, the reluctant, and the mystified. "You've got to be kidding, God. You must have me confused with someone bigger, better, smarter, faster, and more spiritual!"

The reluctance is understandable. Responding to God's call is often costly—emotionally, financially, or even physically. With only a voice from above to guide him, Abram was asked to leave his homeland and his relatives (Gen. 12:1–5). Paul found himself beaten and exposed, attacked and misunderstood when he followed God's call (2 Cor. 11:16–33). Priscilla and Aquila became itinerant church planters, leaving a steady tent-making business behind to join Paul in his missionary work (Acts 18:2, 18–19).

Few of us are asked to make such sacrifices. Our commitment to serve Christ as a coach might require saying no to things we desire to do—playing sports, joining clubs, or relaxing in our favorite chair with a cup of coffee. It may mean organizing a workweek in such a way to free up some time for serving a few small group leaders. The effort to do so is noble, as we come alongside and empower the volunteer shepherds in the body, the small group leaders in our churches.

Ken was a strong, capable small group leader in our church at Willow Creek. He was committed to the men he led and sought to model a vibrant Christian life. When the subject of leadership came up in a conversation, Ken jumped in and shared his desire to see more leaders emerge at Willow. The Holy Spirit was working in Ken, giving him a heart for other leaders. One day we asked him to consider coaching some leaders.

"Wow. You're kidding, right? Did you guys run out of names on your list?"

"No, Ken. Seriously, we see something in you. You have a heart for leaders and a desire to see people grow in Christ. What do you think about mentoring a couple of inexperienced group leaders, helping them work through the challenges they are facing?"

Ken's response was classic. "Here's what I think. Part of me is excited about this new role and responsibility, but the other part is screaming, 'Get out of here now while there's still time!'"

After a few laughs, we challenged Ken to pray, to seek the counsel of others, and to evaluate how he would make this ministry a priority in his schedule. A week later we met again.

"I have to give up the park district basketball league to do this," he said. "But I think that God is in this and I want to move ahead."

"Wasn't that your way of exercising and blowing off a little steam each day?"

"Yes, but as you know, I also have a running partner and can get my exercise with him in the mornings. If I stop playing in the basketball league, that'll open up two nights a week for more time with family, friends, and connecting with small group leaders. And I'll still be able to develop relationships with lost people at work and in the neighborhood. I really want to do this."

Ken did not have to move around the world and sell his possessions, but he had to make some initial sacrifices and reorder his schedule around a call that God was placing on his life. Ken understood that you can't always just add a new calling to your daily routine. *Okay, let me see ... there's the yard to clean up, then a meeting at school, drive Tim to baseball practice, and oh ... what was it? ... I'm forgetting something ... oh yeah, now I remember ... God left a message and I was supposed to call him back as soon as possible.*

Not a chance.

If the coaching role is new to you, and developing leaders places you a bit outside your comfort zone, welcome to the fellowship of the reluctant. Some great names top the list, like Abraham, Moses, Esther, and Paul, who never felt up to the task.

Join the club; none of us is adequate. If you really want to be unnerved, look at the following Bible passages. Each one describes how the apostle Paul often felt unqualified for the task at hand. Each also gives us confidence as we relate our situation to his.

1 Corinthians 9:16: Here, Paul is compelled to fulfill his teaching ministry, saying, "Woe to me if I do not preach the gospel!" A sense of urgency drives him. His task is important to the grander vision of the kingdom of God. So is ours.

2 Corinthians 3:4–6: His competency comes from Christ as he serves in the power of the Spirit. So does ours. We are servants (ministers) of the new covenant, and Christ has made us adequate for the ministry at hand.

2 Corinthians 4:7–12: Though a weak vessel (a fragile, cracked jar of clay), Paul witnesses the life of Christ shining through him so that others can see the power of God. This will be your experience as well.

2 Corinthians 12:7–10: Paul is not disabled by his weaknesses but rather draws strength from Christ in the midst of them. So will you, and you will discover God's grace is sufficient for you.

Few have known the joy and struggle of ministry in a difficult world more than Paul. These passages remind us that it was Christ working in him. We take confidence, therefore, that Christ will work in us as well.

The Need for Coaching

It takes a coach—a shepherd-leader—to build into the lives of small group leaders. The power of the Holy Spirit is released when someone speaks life and hope and truth into the heart of another person. This is especially true for leaders who carry the burden and weight of ministry. They need words of life. Reflecting on the church leader's need for personal, soul-level support and authentic relationships, Larry Crabb writes in *Soul Talk*, "Visionaries call us to religious action. Entrepreneurs figure out how to get the action going. Marketing geniuses brand the action till everybody's talking about it. Gifted performers speak or sing us into action. Again, all good things with an important place—but not first place. More important is that each leader be known by someone, not by a crowd or a committee, but by a person, a close friend, an intimate companion. And not merely held accountable, but genuinely known in an intimate, vulnerable, painfully real, long-term relationship" (p. 53).

Not every coaching relationship will be as deep as Larry longs for and describes. But his point is well taken. Leaders need a person—in our setting, a shepherd-coach—to speak into their lives, to know them, love them, and support them. When this happens, the Holy Spirit seems to stir and awaken the leader. A leader feels cared for and understood, motivated to speak truth and life into those in his or her group. Suddenly, ordinary people have become extraordinary instruments in the hands of God.

The Bible is full of stories that describe what happens when a coach or mentor speaks into the lives of ordinary people, investing in those who show leadership potential.

Moses with Joshua: Feel you are totally unqualified? Consider the classic case of a reluctant leader (Moses) and his young protégé. Together they changed the future of a nation. Moses provided on-the-job training as he mentored Joshua in leading the people of Israel.

Jesus with Peter: Worried about failure and fear? No one failed worse than Peter, who denied his friend and teacher three times in his hour of greatest need. Yet Peter rose past his failures and became the rock-solid foundation of the early church. Learning from a true master of leadership, Peter found encouragement and love from Jesus.

Priscilla and Aquila with Apollos: Intimidated by the prospect of coaching people more gifted than you? Take a good look at this New Testament couple. Recruited by Paul in the business of tent-making, they went on to accompany him in his church-planting ventures. Soon they found themselves coaching the great orator Apollos, a superstar communicator who taught some questionable doctrine. Even though he could teach circles around them, Priscilla and Aquila guided and coached him, releasing him back into ministry.

Paul with Timothy: Feeling weak and timid? Overcome by inexperience? Then you will feel at home in the company of Timothy. Paul's investment in Timothy enabled him to speak courageously in the church at Ephesus at the height of cultural chaos and doctrinal confusion. "Clean up this mess, Timothy!" challenged Paul, and Timothy rose to the occasion.

Even the best leaders need a coach, whether it's Tiger Woods in golf, the Williams sisters in tennis, Jeff Gordon in NASCAR racing, or the successful executives of large corporations. Coaches have a heart for leaders who need encouragement, support, prayer, and a reminder of how important their ministry is to the kingdom. What leader does not need more prayer, love, resources, and encouragement? Leaders need a person to speak into their lives, and that person is you!

Fostering a Development Mindset

Coaches are experts at helping others shine. Who do you think is the better golfer, Tiger Woods or his coach? Who is the better tennis player, Serena Williams or her coach? Who is the better race car driver, Jeff Gordon or his team manager? Who is the better CEO, the personal life coach or the person actually leading IBM or Shell or Microsoft? You get the idea. Coaches are not necessarily the world's best small group leaders. Coaches find joy in helping others become great small group leaders. For a coach, personal success is found in releasing others to succeed.

Paul was certainly a gifted church planter and developer of leaders. Look at some of his work with Timothy as an example of the developmental mindset every coach needs.

Reflections

Take a moment to consider your reaction to what you have been reading. Perhaps this is a time for some dialogue with God. It might sound like this: "God, I still feel a bit overwhelmed. I believe that you have worked in others. Scripture is clear about that. You have promised to use me despite my weaknesses. You will provide the spiritual and emotional resources I need to face my fear. But I confess I still feel a bit reluctant. Please meet me here and help me to trust your power."

This might be a good time to contact others who have been called to ministry roles that required them to step outside their comfort zones. Talk to other coaches, small group leaders, staff members, or board members at your church. Ask them some questions about their journey into ministry.

1. What were their fears?
2. How did God provide grace to meet such fears?
3. What were the rewards?
4. How did they grow spiritually in the process of taking this risk into a new area of ministry?

Doing Ministry through Others: Honoring the Priesthood of Believers

Peter's writings provide a clear picture of our role as believers in Christ. In 1 Peter 2:9, he writes, "But you are a chosen people, a royal priesthood, a holy nation, God's special possession, that you may declare the praises of him who called you out of darkness into his wonderful light."

Yes. You and I are a royal priesthood, given the privileges and responsibilities of carrying out the ministry of Christ. Unlike Old Testament–era priests, we do not wear elaborate robes or sacrifice animals at an altar. Instead of serving in the temple we are called to communicate the message that Jesus Christ became the supreme sacrifice for us (Heb. 9:27–28). Our bodies—not buildings—are temples of the Holy Spirit (1 Cor. 3:16–17). We offer a new kind of sacrifice, our lives in service to Christ (Rom. 12:1–2). We have been entrusted with ministry to build up the body of Christ (Eph. 4:16).

So be encouraged. God has asked you to participate in the adventure of serving, celebrating, supporting, and developing leaders for his community. Ministry is not something you hold on to like an old pair of jeans, useful only to you. It was meant to be shared with others so that the effects and impact can be multiplied. The joy of ministering to group members through small group leaders is what makes coaching so rewarding. A coach may influence two, three, or even more group leaders, who in turn affect the lives of twenty or thirty people. The impact your ministry has on a few multiplies into the hearts of many.

Part Two

The Essence of Coaching

What does it take to become an effective coach? What is at the very core of the coaching enterprise?

Baseball players call them the fundamentals of the game. Bank managers call them sound business practices. Whether it is playing baseball or managing a bank, certain core values shape the heart of every enterprise. The same is true of coaching leaders. Certain core values and essential characteristics define the ministry. These must be embraced, developed, and nurtured over time.

Embrace a Vision for Transformation

We hope that every coach and every small group leader shares the same passion —to see people grow into the image of Christ. If a leader doesn't share this passion, something is wrong. Paul, one of the supreme models for coaching in the Bible, yearned to see his "children" grow in Christ. It was a driving passion in his life and often moved him deeply. "My dear children, for whom I am again in the pains of childbirth until Christ is formed in you ..." (Gal. 4:19).

That is the compelling vision we must embrace and share. But unfortunately, not every small group leader views their group with such focus. Some who lack this vision, or who are ignorant of the potential for God to change a life, simply approach it as a social gathering. After a few jokes, some snacks, and a discussion about the new kitchen cabinets or latest football scores, everyone says a brief prayer and goes home. Other leaders may grasp a vision for supporting people in pain, but they never go beyond discussing the wounds and scars of life. People nod their heads in sympathy, offer prayers for healing, and the meeting comes to a close. Some group leaders may view the group as a teaching center, with them as the teacher. After an extended explanation of the Bible passage, a brief discussion ensues. The conversation is content-heavy and opinion-oriented, filled with members' comments, like, "That's interesting." "I never knew that before." "I disagree with that interpretation." Well-meaning and thorough, this leader is committed to the Bible—which is good. But this leader also thinks that simply teaching and debating the content of the Bible is the purpose of the group.

The vision for transformation transcends discussion of Bible content. Changed lives are at the heart of the vision. All other aspects of group life—including social interaction, compassion for one another, and Bible discussion—contribute to an atmosphere for transformation but are never sufficient in themselves. Transformation takes place in the heart, resulting in attitudes, thoughts, and behaviors becoming like those of the Master, Jesus. Group leaders and coaches alike must embrace such a vision, because it is God's vision. "It is enough for students to be like their teacher, and servants like their master," said Jesus (Matt. 10:25). Being like the Master is the goal of all group members.

Believe People Can Change

Bill Hybels is senior pastor at Willow Creek Community Church in suburban Chicago. For years, one of the core values at Willow Creek has been a passion to see people transformed into fully devoted followers of Jesus Christ. Early in his ministry, an older man pulled young Hybels aside after a service, hoping to save the twenty-three-year-old pastor from disappointments in ministry.

"Hey Bill. You're an idealistic young guy, but can I shoot straight with you? You stand up there each week preaching your heart out, hoping people will change. But the truth is, people just don't change." Hybels replied with courage and conviction, "Well, sir, I'm betting my whole life on the fact that you are wrong."

How would you respond to the same challenge? Are you passionate about transformation? Do you believe that people can and do change in response to the work of the Holy Spirit in them? Do you believe that they are not yet what God wants them to be, despite what they look like on the surface? Can you look past their inadequacies, failures, quirks, and inexperience to see what they can become by the grace of God? Can you help a leader extract the gold that is hidden deep within, waiting to be mined by someone who takes the time to believe in them?

Trust the Work of the Holy Spirit

You are not the agent of spiritual growth in a person; that is the job of the Holy Spirit at work in you and in your leaders. So take confidence in the fact that your labor is not in vain. God is at work through you and in them. This takes a lot of pressure off of each of us who coaches others. Our responsibility is to inspire, pray, encourage, and challenge, but God causes the growth. Listen to these words from 1 Corinthians reminding us that the Spirit of God is doing his work in us.

> My message and my preaching were not with wise and persuasive words, but with a demonstration of the Spirit's power, so that your faith might not rest on human wisdom, but on God's power.   —1 Corinthians 2:4–5

> The Spirit searches all things, even the deep things of God ... We have not received the spirit of the world but the Spirit who is from God, that we may understand what God has freely given us.   —1 Corinthians 2:10, 12

> I planted the seed, Apollos watered it, but God has been making it grow. So neither the one who plants nor the one who waters is anything, but only God, who makes things grow.   —1 Corinthians 3:6–7

Aren't you relieved that we are not responsible for people's growth? The Holy Spirit is the agent of change. God simply asks us to create an environment that nurtures that growth. We plant seeds of truth and we "plant" new leaders in the soil and support of the Christian community. We provide resources, pray prayers, and connect people with teaching that will feed them and allow their roots to grow deep. The community of believers and other growing leaders will nurture this new plant and provide wisdom and counsel. The water of the Word of God will shape and transform character traits, beliefs, and attitudes. And we as coaches have the joy of watching the plant mature into a healthy, fruit-bearing tree, by God's grace. So take confidence, the Holy Spirit is at work in you!

Remember That God Will Use You

God can and will use you. Never tire of working on behalf of your leaders, because God is working through you to impact others, though this influence may not be apparent at first. Here are a few ways that he is using you.

Modeling: What you do and how you do it is an example to your leaders, so continue to pursue Christ and live with integrity (1 Cor. 11:1).

Words: What you say can build up or tear down (James 3). "A word aptly spoken is like apples of gold in settings of silver," says Proverbs 25:11.

Prayer: God delayed the movement of the sun and stopped the falling of the rain in response to prayer. (See Joshua 10:13 and 1 Kings 17:1; 18:41–44). He acts and moves as we pray according to his will.

Listening: Listening to your leaders with empathy and intention will show them you care about them as people, not just as names on the organizational chart in your church (James 1:19).

Nurture Your Love of Community

"Community," exhorted Dietrich Bonhoeffer, "is what we share in Christ" and is not something we create. Community is created by God; we are called to *participate* in this reality. First Corinthians 12 declares that at the moment of our conversion and our adoption, we are baptized into a body, a community. We often fail to realize this. Our focus tends to be on the personal and individual aspects of our salvation; however, we need to tell new followers of Christ that they are part of a holy community, the church, the body of Christ. One reason we promote and practice small group life is to connect people to a place in the body where they can live out the reality of their individual *and* their communal relationships to God through Christ.

Coaches develop and support group leaders because they "are devoted to the fellowship" and long for others to experience the gift of community. Maybe you have led or have been in small groups, and you know what life in community can be like. Now, as a shepherd of small group leaders, you have the opportunity to give the gift of community to other leaders and to watch them share this gift with their groups.

They devoted themselves to the apostles' teaching and to the fellowship, to the breaking of bread and to prayer.

—Acts 2:42

Questions for Reflection

1. Do you remember when you first experienced true community? What did it look like and feel like?
2. What can you do to help those you shepherd understand this gift of community?

Cultivate a Passion for Developing Leaders

A major barrier to spiritual growth and the connection of people in the church community is the availability and empowerment of shepherd-leaders who will nurture them in Christ and provide a safe, loving place for them to belong. What shepherd-leaders do is inspire and support people who have been called to lead a small community. Jesus Christ, working through his body, the church, is the hope of the world, and the church's future rests in the hands of capable shepherd-leaders who will guide others toward growth.

Ministry is like love—it has no value if it is hoarded. The point is to give it away. As you empower and encourage leaders, you are giving ministry into their hands, placing them on the front lines of effective shepherding. It is a ministry of reproduction. Few people have modeled this ministry more effectively at Willow Creek than Mark Weinert.

During the 1980s, Mark led the small groups ministry at the church, pouring his life into coaches and leaders alike. In 1992, he left the staff to take a seat on our board and return to the marketplace. Discipleship was never a position for Mark; it was a way of life. It made no difference where his paycheck came from. He simply invested in people and continues to do so to this day.

To honor Mark, in 1992 we invited him in front of the congregation to thank him for his efforts on the church staff. So that he could see the impact of his work, we asked members of the congregation to stand if they had been personally discipled by Mark, either in a small group or one-on-one. Fifteen people stood up. Then we asked people to look carefully at those standing. "If you were discipled by anyone who is standing, please rise." Another forty to fifty people stood up. It was very impressive. Finally, a third request. "If you have been discipled by any of the people who just stood up, please stand." By now, there were at least two hundred people standing, the fruit of three generations of leadership and discipleship. Many were small group leaders and coaches. The sight moved us all deeply, and Mark was quite overwhelmed at the number who stood, many of whom he did not know personally.

The power of God working in one life has a ripple effect, reproducing fruit in each generation of leadership. When coaches have a passion to develop and support a leader, that leader will impact the lives of people in the small group they lead. And on it goes, like ripples traveling far beyond their point of origin in a tranquil lake. The ministry of coaching has the same incredible opportunity and potential.

Your Impact in the Life of a Leader

Coaches for life-change can help small group leaders in two major ways:

1. Coaches help leaders *define their expectations* for leadership and small group community life.
2. Coaches create a healthy level of *support and accountability* for the development and progress of leaders.

Often, group leaders are not sure they are being effective when they lead a small community. The development of people is hard work, and the fruit of their labors may not be seen for weeks, months—even years. Knowing what defines true success and who is going to provide the support and care they need along the way is important for leaders.

Setting Expectations for the Coach-Leader Relationship

What Do Leaders Expect from Coaches?

1. Provide support and care
2. Make a commitment to the person, not the position
3. Create an environment of trust

What Do Coaches Expect from Leaders?

1. Fulfill their responsibilities as a leader
2. Maintain truthful communication
3. Maintain a humble, teachable spirit

And the things you have heard me say in the presence of many witnesses entrust to reliable people who will also be qualified to teach others.
—2 Timothy 2:2

Develop the Heart of a Shepherd

The biblical description of a shepherd is a proactive and engaging one. God lays out the marks of a shepherd in some key Bible passages.

In Psalm 23, a shepherd:
- Guides to rest and refreshment
- Comforts in the face of difficulty
- Provides for life
- Assures of God's presence

In Ezekiel 34:11–16, a shepherd:
- Leads the sheep to places of rest
- Feeds the sheep
- Searches for the lost
- Brings back the strays
- Binds up the weak

In John 10:7–18, a shepherd:
- Provides protection
- Is willing to make sacrifices for the sheep
- Is committed to the well-being of the flock

This list is not exhaustive, nor do we present it to overwhelm you. Rather, it provides insight into the true heart of a shepherd—what he or she should be focused on when encouraging and supporting leaders.

Few coaches embody the characteristics described above more than Debbie Beise. She was a great coach because she had a great heart for leaders. Typically, coaches gather with their leaders every four to six weeks. Debbie met with hers weekly—because they wanted to! Though she suffered from liver cancer, she courageously devoted herself to her leaders, many of whom fought serious challenges of their own and needed care and support.

Some Next Steps to Consider

How You Can Develop Your Vision, Passion, and Heart

1. Come alongside an existing coach or experienced leader of leaders (a staff member at the church, for example). Watch how they deal with people and ask if you can help.

2. Pray for God to give you the mind of a shepherd.

3. Take a specific interest in a leader you know, seeking to serve them and pray for them. Visit with that leader and discover their needs. Seek to help them in some way.

4. Read the passages about shepherding carefully and allow the Spirit to teach you. Are there areas you are neglecting as you care for leaders? How are you getting to know the sheep in your flock? What opportunities exist for getting to know them and their needs?

5. Spend time with others whom you consider to be good shepherds.

Part Three

A Coach's Key Practices

Bob has been a coach of small group leaders for several years. He loves God and loves spending time with those he coaches. They seem to have a good relationship with him. Yet both Bob and his leaders are frustrated. Something is missing. The groups are not growing, the leaders feel inadequate, and Bob is considering stepping down as a coach.

Mary's groups are thriving. Stories of life-change seem to come to her on a weekly basis —both from her leaders and from their groups. Though conflicts and problems arise, they never seem to derail the progress of the groups. Her leaders eagerly anticipate time together. Mary seems to be the poster child for coaching.

What is the difference between Bob's and Mary's coaching? What makes one coach successful and another not? Often the difference can be narrowed to a handful of skills that a coach practices regularly. In this part, we will look at four key practices for coaching, and how you can use them to grow in your ministry.

The Big Picture

Four key skills can determine a coach's effectiveness. Take heart—you don't need to be perfect at them, nor is proficiency a prerequisite to becoming a coach. You can learn and develop all four over time. In reality, each coach will be stronger in some of these practices and weaker in others. To be effective in your ministry simply requires that you continue to grow in each area.

The key practices for coaches are as follows:

Equipping: Develop Skills

Provide training in key skills so that leaders become more effective in meeting the real needs of group members.

Their responsibility is to equip God's people to do his work and build up the church, the body of Christ (Eph. 4:12 NLT).

Envisioning: Dream Together

Imagine with your leaders how their group could impact group members, the church, and the community.

When dreams come true, there is life and joy (Prov. 13:12 NLT).

Guiding: Shepherd Intentionally

Help your leaders identify and take their next step in spiritual growth.

Patiently correct, rebuke, and encourage your people (2 Tim. 4:2 NLT).

Modeling: Pursue Christ-likeness

Grow in the life of full devotion you're inviting others to lead.

Follow my example, just as I follow Christ's (1 Cor. 11:1 NLT).

These skills build in progression, one upon the other, like stair steps. The coaching relationship starts with modeling a God-honoring life. All other practices rest on this foundation.

After modeling, coaches then add the practice of guiding, but they never stop modeling. To skip or abandon any level will create problems. To ignore guiding and move straight to envisioning or equipping leaders can bring the feeling of mid-level management to the coaching relationship.

This progression continues to envisioning and equipping, moving upward as trust grows between the leader and coach. Let's look at each step in greater depth.

Key Practice 1

Modeling: Pursue Christ-likeness

The best way coaches can motivate their leaders to live a God-honoring, Christ-centered life is to model that life for them. Without pride or arrogance, simply live the kind of life that God calls us to live, "in such a way that no one will be hindered from finding the Lord by the way we act, and so no one can find fault with our ministry" (2 Cor. 6:3 NLT).

Jesus taught that when modeling is working as it should, the disciple will ultimately become like his teacher (Luke 6:40). Leadership studies have shown this to be true. They confirm that in about thirty-six months, the people you lead will very closely reflect who you are. A loving teacher will produce loving disciples. A joyful teacher typically has disciples who are filled with joy.

The sobering aspect of this principle is that it works whether the values and practices the teacher models are good or bad. Therefore it is critical that you model the right pattern of living for your leaders.

On the surface, modeling can feel haughty or arrogant. Who am I to say that people should follow my example of Christian living?

On a number of occasions Paul asked—even commanded—others to follow his example. Listen to Paul's coaching to three different churches:

- Therefore I urge you to imitate me. Follow my example, as I follow the example of Christ (1 Cor. 4:16; 11:1).
- Join together in following my example (Phil. 3:17).
- For you yourselves know how you ought to follow our example (2 Thess. 3:7).

Paul invested his life in Timothy and Titus, two young men he coached in ministry. He encouraged them to follow his lead and model the Christian life for those in their care (1 Tim. 4:12; Titus 2:7).

Yet if you scan the book of Acts, you will quickly see that Paul was no angel. He had his flaws and shortcomings, and he was human, just like us. So how did Paul, and how can we, resolve the tension between the reality of our spiritual condition and calling others to follow our example?

By being real—by sharing what God is doing in your life right now. The key practice of modeling is not about being perfect. Even as Paul was encouraging the Christians at Philippi to follow his example, he confessed his weaknesses to them. "I'm not saying that I have this all together, that I have it made. But I am well on my way, reaching out for Christ, who has so wondrously reached out for me. Friends, don't get me wrong: By no means do I count myself an expert in all of this, but I've got my eye on the goal" (Phil. 3:12–13 MSG).

This is where good coaching begins. Authentically modeling the life to which God calls us.

Leaders lead not by merit of temperament or gifts, but by living a life that is so compellingly like Christ that others naturally want to follow them. To follow them to Christ.

—Joseph Stowell,
Shepherding the Church into the Twenty-First Century

People do what people see. Modeling provides the basis of all true leadership, and leaders must set an example for their followers.

—John Maxwell,
"Becoming a Spiritual Role Model"

Common Error

Coaches often downplay the effect that their life and example can have on small group leaders. You are an example to them. What you do and how you live your life has a powerful impact. That's why Paul said to Timothy, "Set an example for the believers in speech, in conduct, in love, in faith, and in purity" (1 Tim. 4:12). Paul knew the principles of Christian living are not only taught, they are caught. Knowledge and skill combined with the example of your own life has a transforming effect on your group leaders.

Model Spirit-Filled Leadership

When the early church needed new leaders, they carefully and prayerfully selected believers who had evidenced certain qualities—a faith firmly grounded in God's Word, a life showing solid character, and a heart filled with the Holy Spirit and wisdom (Acts 6:1–7). As you follow the lives and ministries of these leaders, you quickly see that their leadership was indeed Spirit-filled.

A coach's life and leadership needs to model these same qualities. The challenge of coaching small group leaders demands you lean into the wisdom of God's Word and the power of the Holy Spirit. Coaches will not accomplish their ministry through their own might or power. Ministry can only be done through the strength and the power given to them by God's Holy Spirit (Zech. 4:6).

We are tempted to rely on our own skills, abilities, and experiences. While these will serve you well as a coach, they are not enough. This kind of Spirit-less leadership will eventually leave coaches at the end of their resources. They will eventually mishandle challenges and overlook growth opportunities for the leaders in their care.

Follow the example of Jesus and learn to live and lead by the Spirit. Allow him to direct your ministry.

Model Spiritual Fitness

America is a health-crazed nation. Billions of dollars are spent each year on physical fitness—health club memberships, home fitness machines, and fitness apparel. Coaches need to approach spiritual fitness with the same intensity and energy.

Coaches would do well to heed Paul's advice to his protégé, Timothy: "Take the time and trouble to keep yourself spiritually fit" (1 Tim. 4:16 Phillips). Take time to develop a spiritual life that is vibrant, healthy, and growing.

Your spiritual life is the foundation upon which you build your ministry. Pay careful attention to your personal relationship with Christ and how you model that relationship for your leaders. The level of success you have in the other three key practices depends upon the foundation you build in the practice of modeling.

You will spend much of your time as a coach investing in relationships with people. You will be giving, sharing, leading, teaching, guiding, envisioning, equipping, and shepherding. It is important for you to regularly set aside time alone with God, time where he is feeding and building into you. Here are a few spiritual disciplines that are key for ongoing spiritual fitness.

The great apostle Paul lived with the constant awareness that his failure to manage his inner life well could actually result in his own personal stumbling, thus negatively affecting all he had worked so hard to accomplish as an apostle.

—Samuel Rima,
Leading from the Inside Out

Bible Study

Eugene Peterson, a seasoned shepherd of his flock, has said that two of the things he neglected most in ministry were prayer and personal Bible reading. Without them, the personal growth of the leader is stunted.

In Psalm 19:7–9 David tells us that God's Word will:

- Refresh our soul
- Make even the simple wise
- Give joy to the heart
- Give light to the eyes

What coach doesn't need that? But what kind of Bible reading will feed and nurture your soul? At its core, personal Bible study needs to be about simply spending time with God, building and nurturing your relationship with him. Unhurried chunks of time spent washing your mind in God's Word.

Ordering our lives to spend time with Christ is not easy. Time with God is often the first thing we neglect when confronted with a busy schedule. You will have to be persistent to schedule time in order to cultivate a deeper relationship with Christ.

Approach your personal Bible study using these simple guidelines:

1. Make an appointment with God. If it is helpful, write in your PDA or calendar the time and location when you will meet with God.
2. Find a quiet place, free from distractions.
3. Take a couple of deep breaths to still yourself from the events and activities of your day, those already passed and those yet to come.
4. Begin with a simple prayer, such as, "Lord, speak to me through your Word today. I am listening."
5. Remember the focus is your personal relationship with God. Resist the temptation to look for something to give to your leaders. Let God fill *you* and speak *to you*.
6. Read slowly—allowing the truth to wash over you. When a verse or phrase catches your attention, stop and think about the implications of that passage for your life (meditate on it).

Prayer

Prayer was a regular part of Jesus' life. Mark tells us in his gospel, "Very early in the morning, while it was still dark, Jesus got up, left the house and went off to a solitary place, where he prayed" (Mark 1:35).

Regular communication with his Father was a source of strength, comfort, and guidance for Christ. He spent time in prayer following successful ministry (Mark 1:35), in advance of difficult challenges (John 17), and prior to making major decisions (Luke 6:12–13). It's safe to say that Jesus prayed continually (1 Thess. 5:17).

Prayer can be a source of strength, comfort, and guidance for coaches as well. Set aside regular time to communicate with God about:

- Your own spiritual development. What are your growth edges? What are the struggles and sins that continually trip you up? What recent spiritual growth can you celebrate?

- Areas where you need God's guidance and direction
- The spiritual growth of your leaders
- Needs, issues, and problems you and your leaders are facing

Worship

It was Jesus' custom to regularly participate in corporate worship (Luke 4:16). Worship offers us a chance to give God the glory and honor that is due him (Ps. 29:2). Personal and corporate worship fills the soul in a way few spiritual disciplines can. When our heart is right, we approach worship with gladness and joy (Ps. 100:2), not as a duty to be fulfilled. The hearts of believers should long to meet with God in worship (Ps. 42).

At a minimum, coaches should regularly attend the worship services of their church. In addition, set aside time for worship in other settings. The possibilities include:

- Using worship music as a part of your daily commute
- Worshiping with your small group
- Beginning or ending your leadership huddles with worship
- Including worship as a part of your quiet time

Solitude

According to Kenneth Boa, solitude is simply "time deliberately spent away from interaction with other people to nurture depth, perspective, purpose, and resolve."

As we read the Gospels we see that Jesus regularly practiced this discipline of solitude. Doing so allowed him to escape the pressure, noise, and distraction of daily life. It allowed him to connect deeply with God and to make certain his ministry was guided by the Spirit rather than by selfish desires or external expectations.

Solitude, often practiced in conjunction with the discipline of silence, causes us to slow down, to allow Jesus room to roam in our life and ministry. It allows us to truly pray, as David did, "Examine me, GOD, from head to foot, order your battery of tests. Make sure I'm fit inside and out so I never lose sight of your love, but keep in step with you, never missing a beat" (Ps. 26:2–3 MSG).

Solitude creates space for us to listen to God. God often speaks to us in a whisper. If there's too much noise or too many distractions, we can easily miss him.

Look for pockets of solitude in your daily life, like during your work commute or lunch hour. Use this time to experiment with solitude. Spend it in silence, alone with God.

Longer blocks of time spent in solitude will require more planning. Look ahead in your calendar and block out a time for extended solitude, preferably a full day. Doing this on a monthly or quarterly basis will deepen your connection with Christ and bear fruit in your life and ministry.

Modeling Community

It is vital that coaches remain actively connected to community in a small group. As odd as it seems, it is not uncommon for coaches to get so involved in mentoring leaders and building a small group ministry that they are no longer personally involved in a small group.

Coaches need to model a vital connection to community for two reasons:

- Integrity demands that those who are building community be living in it. It is difficult to cast a credible vision for community if you are not personally living out the vision.
- A connection to community is vital to the personal spiritual health of a coach.

For many coaches, the time demands of coaching require that they step out of their leadership role in a small group. Leaving the community where they know and are known, love and are loved, serve and are served, celebrate and are celebrated raises an important issue: Where do coaches find community?

Some coaches are able to navigate the transition from being the leader to simply being a member in their current group. If remaining in your current group is not a viable option, pursue a new group. Seek out a small group where you are given the gift of being yourself, where you are viewed as a group member and not a "small group expert."

Because they share the same dream and vision for community, coaches and leaders can often establish a deep relational and spiritual connection in their leadership huddle times (see part 4: "The Coach's Toolbox" for a detailed explanation of leadership huddles). As in any small group, this community will take time and intentionality to develop. If you desire your huddles to function as a community, lead them accordingly.

Depending on your church's small group structure, you may also find your community needs are met when the coaches gather for vision and training. Yet in order to meet the need for community, these leadership huddles need to be more than business meetings.

Moving into the role of coach may provide the opportunity for you to pursue a new type of community. In this season you may want to consider pursuing community with a spiritual mentor or friend.

Time for a Checkup

Too often life becomes routine, and our spiritual disciplines can easily become part of that routine. How do we break out of this? Take a few moments right now and assess your personal spiritual condition by reflecting on these questions.

Spirit-Filled Leadership

1. Think back over the last six months. Using the image from Zechariah 4:6, has your leadership been more by might and power, or by the Spirit?

2. What is one step you could take to move toward spiritual leadership?

Spiritual Fitness

1. What is the condition of your soul right now, fit or flabby?

2. Which of the four disciplines discussed (Bible study, prayer, worship, or solitude) do you sense God might be asking you to pursue or deepen?

3. How could you begin to pursue or deepen this discipline?

Community

1. Where and with whom are you connecting in community?

2. What steps can you take to move into deeper levels of community in those settings?

Feedback

1. Who knows you well enough that they can speak truth into your life in these areas of disciplines? (List these people below.)

2. When can you meet with one or more of them to seek their insight?

Key Practice 2

Guiding: Shepherd Intentionally

Most of the leaders you serve have a vision for their group. They have a picture in their head of where they want to lead their group. Some leaders have a macro-level vision—a general sense of how they want people to develop a deeper relationship with God and with the members of the group. For others, the vision is more on the micro level—they have a detailed plan of growth for individual members of the group.

Most of the leaders you serve are self-motivated. They have a passion for community and that drives them to build relationships and to lead their groups. They are self-starters and self-sustainers.

What leaders need is a guide—someone to help refine their goals and sharpen their vision. The apostle Paul served in this role for Timothy and Silas, two of his leaders-in-training. His working relationship with them was so strong that it's referenced nineteen times in the New Testament.

Paul played a significant part in launching their ministries throughout Asia. The fingerprints of Paul's shepherding relationships were all over their ministry. Due in part to the careful guidance they received from Paul, Timothy and Silas saw tremendous results from their ministry efforts.

Both newly commissioned and seasoned leaders need a coach who will serve as a guide for them. They need someone who will listen and intentionally explore the work of God in them. They need someone who will help them identify and take their next steps of spiritual growth and leadership development. They need someone who will intentionally shepherd them.

Taking on the role of guide for small group leaders may elicit concerns and fears.

- *What if I can't answer their leadership questions?* No coach has the answer to every question about group life. Simply admit you don't know and then work together to find the solution.
- *How can I offer spiritual guidance when I struggle too?* Seldom is a coach a spiritual giant. Effective shepherds simply offer wisdom and counsel from their experiences. They seek out help when they don't know the answers.
- *How long will I serve as a guide?* Seldom does a coach guide a leader from conversion to death. More typically they guide a leader for one leg of the journey, one step at a time.
- *What if the leader doesn't want to grow or develop spiritually?* You are not responsible for anyone's spiritual development except your own. Coaches cannot make people grow. Your responsibility is to challenge and provide encouragement and the opportunity for growth. The leaders will choose to grow or not.

- *What about serious issues—ones I may not be equipped to handle?* Remember, you are called to be a guide, not a counselor. Know when to refer to a staff member or counselor in your area.
- *Am I being asked to be a spiritual director for my leaders?* Your role will more closely resemble a spiritual friend than a spiritual director.

Common Error

Coaches can easily miss the need to build community with and among their leaders. They move too quickly to envisioning and equipping their leaders. While these are great steps (in fact they are our next two key practices), placing an emphasis on them too early in the coach/leader relationship is not good.

When this happens, leaders can be left feeling that they have a manager or director, not a guide. A manager will check in on the goals, assessing and rewarding progress. When this happens to group leaders it can leave them feeling like they are simply the middle rung in a multilevel marketing firm with an eternal product.

As a guide, coaches place a high value on shepherding their leaders. They will provide a safe community where leaders can confess their struggles without feeling like a failure and where they can celebrate successes without feeling like they are boasting. A community where leaders can explore next steps in their spiritual growth and their group leadership. A guide honors the journey as much as the final destination.

Relationships First

Jesus placed a high priority on relationships in his ministry. He built strong relationships during the time spent with the Twelve. That was Jesus' plan from the beginning. Consider the relational component in these passages:

Mark 3:14: Jesus calls the Twelve for two purposes: to be with him and to do ministry. The first priority was relationships—the "be-with" factor. One translation says Jesus called them to be his "regular companions."

John 14:3: To calm their fears, Jesus assures the Twelve that he will return for them one day. Why? So they can "be with" him.

John 15:15: At the Last Supper, Jesus says, "I no longer call you servants … instead, I have called you friends."

John 17:24: Just hours before his death, Jesus prays in the garden. One of his deepest longings is for the Twelve to "be with" him again in heaven.

Forming an authentic relationship is the first step to intentionally shepherding your leaders. Leaders want to be built into, cared for, and loved. Leaders want to establish trust, open communication, and form genuine relationships. They first want to have a shepherd who feeds them rather than a supervisor who leads them.

Over the years, this principle has been proven time and again at Willow Creek. It is often referred to as the "feed/lead ratio." Leaders consistently express a desire to be "fed" by their coaches. They primarily desire a shepherd who cares for them. They want a coach who seeks to understand them—their personal walk with God, their family life, their relationship to the church. One who helps them discern next steps of personal spiritual growth.

I am the good shepherd; I know my sheep and my sheep know me.
—Jesus, John 10:14

Nothing can substitute for personal time with each member of your flock! It will be in such private times that you will discern their value systems and deepest needs … there will be times when more private sessions will help you gain special insights into each person.
—Ralph Neighbour, *The Shepherd's Guidebook*

More than thirty years after beginning this journey into community as a church, our leaders still desire shepherding. A recent survey of group leaders confirmed this fact. Leaders want a coach who knows them like a shepherd knows his sheep.

Initially, at least, leaders are looking for this feeding aspect to comprise about 80 percent of the coach/leader relationship. The other 20 percent is leadership, providing the vision and the skills necessary to carry out the role of group leader. Over time you will see this ratio begin to shift. As trust builds, the leadership component can increase substantially, but never to the point that it outweighs the shepherding component.

It will take time and intentionality to develop a relationship with each of your leaders. A coach needs to consistently seek to understand the whole picture of who each one is, both as a person and as a leader. As you build trust with the leader, ask deeper questions that uncover their thoughts, beliefs, and feelings. Ask questions that will help you:

> *Understand their spiritual journey.* How did they come to Christ? To your church? Who has been influential in their journey?

> *Understand their life history.* What was/is their family like? How did they celebrate? Grieve? How did they handle conflict? What were the major turning points in their life?

> *Understand their heart.* What brings them joy? What makes them sad? What do they dream about?

While the primary tool to build relationships will be one-on-one time, you can also plan activities to foster relationships with your leaders during huddle times. (For ideas on how to utilize each of these settings, see part 4: "The Coach's Toolbox.")

Listen Deeply

Whether the conversation is a planned one-on-one time or a chance meeting, coaches need to practice good listening skills. As you shepherd your leaders, here are some guidelines:

- *Listen more than you speak.* Don't interrupt or look for openings in the conversation to get your point across. "Everyone should be quick to listen, slow to speak and slow to become angry" (James 1:19).
- *Actively engage in their story.* As leaders share their story, do not become preoccupied with pondering your next question or response.
- *Ask for clarification.* When what they are communicating is not clear to you, don't presume to know what they are trying to say.
- *Keep the focus on them.* Resist the urge to use their story as a springboard to tell your experiences. Use your stories and experiences sparingly and only when doing so would be helpful to the leader's growth.
- *Fight the temptation to move too quickly to solutions.* Seek to listen and fully understand. "Answering before listening is both stupid and rude" (Prov. 18:13 MSG).
- *Listen beyond their words.* Watch their body language, facial expressions, tone of voice, and choice of words. These nonverbal cues can help you discern unexpressed thoughts, feelings, and struggles.

Being heard is so close to being loved that for the average person they are almost indistinguishable.
—David Augsburger,
Caring Enough to Hear and Be Heard

- *Ask permission to move deeper.* Ask questions that get beyond surface conversation and offer the opportunity to share feelings, opinions, and values. Try to move from self-description to self-disclosure.
- *When your mind wanders, confess it.* Everyone has those moments when their mind drifts. Generally people can tell if you are not really listening. When it happens to you, honestly tell the leader, ask them to forgive you, and encourage them to repeat what they shared.

Be an Encourager

Leading a group can be a rewarding experience. Leaders help people form new friendships and they watch those relationships grow. They see people come to Christ and grow in their devotion to him. They develop and launch new leaders.

But group leadership can also be very challenging. What seem like fantastic plans for a group meeting may flop. Members will miss meetings. People work late, they take vacations, or their kids get sick. At times, relational harmony will give way to chaos. Conflict will happen. Group members will move away or quit. Groups birth. Groups end. Some group members grow spiritually while some seem to grow stagnant.

In the tough times, a word of encouragement can mean the difference between a leader staying in the game or quitting. The truth is, we all need encouragement. That's how God wired us.

Throughout Scripture, good leaders have modeled this need for us:
- At God's command, Moses encouraged his apprentice, Joshua (Deut. 1:38; 3:28).
- King Hezekiah encouraged those who were giving their lives in service to the Lord (2 Chron. 30:22).
- Josiah encouraged the spiritual leaders of Israel (2 Chron. 35:2).
- A major portion of Paul's writing and ministry to churches was encouragement (Acts 14:22; 16:40; 20:1–2; 27:36).
- One leader, Joseph, did this so well that the apostles gave him a new name: Barnabas (Acts 4:36). Literally translated it means "son of encouragement." Later we find him living up to the new name as he encouraged the churches (Acts 11:23).

Leaders need their coach to be a Barnabas for them. They need encouragement to continue to grow spiritually, and they need you to offer words of encouragement on a regular basis. Leaders have expressed that what they desire most from their coach is spiritual development skills. Gain their permission and their trust to serve as a guide—not an expert—for the next leg of their spiritual journey, and check in with them regularly regarding their personal spiritual growth.

- In what disciplines and practices are your leaders regularly engaging?
- Have they drifted away from God? At times we all stray and need a guiding hand and loving encouragement to return to God.
- Where do they sense God is leading them to grow next? Help them discern what their growth edges could be.
- What could a next step of spiritual growth look like? Rather than tell them what to do, brainstorm a list of possibilities. Explore together what new spiritual disciplines or practices could help their growth.

A coach who encourages can make the difference between success and failure, between the leader continuing and giving up.
—Joel Comiskey,
How to Be a Great Cell Group Coach

Beyond guidance in spiritual growth, group leaders need encouragement in their group leadership skills. They need a coach who will:

- Offer encouragement for things they have done well, even little things.
- Praise them when they tackle difficult issues and challenges. Even though they may not complete every detail perfectly, find the things leaders do well and offer genuine praise.
- Encourage them to persevere in the tough times and not get tired of doing the right things. They'll see the benefits in time if they don't get discouraged and give up (Gal. 6:9).
- Use a variety of encouragement styles. Personally written letters, cards, and even email notes are a great source of encouragement to leaders. Recognition in front of their peers can also be important.
- Discover their unique leadership gifts and potential.
- When appropriate, offer public praise or even awards. A great time for this is in your leadership huddles. Sharing the struggles and successes your leaders experience can deepen community and cast vision for the kind of groups and leaders you hope to build.

Most change happens slowly, over time. So as you encourage growth in your leaders, remember Paul's words: "Be prepared in season and out of season; correct, rebuke and encourage—with great patience and careful instruction" (2 Tim. 4:2).

A Caring Shepherd

A tender, compassionate heart is a key facet of intentional shepherding. God described his heart for shepherding in Ezekiel 34. Key responsibilities of a shepherd are:

- Strengthening the weak
- Healing the sick
- Binding up the injured
- Bringing back the strays
- Searching for the lost

Your leaders will eventually encounter pain, loss, and disappointment in their own lives or in the life of a group member. In those seasons, leaders may need guidance from you. They may need help determining how best to care for group members who are in crisis. This is especially true for:

- Leaders who have never walked through a crisis with a group
- Newly formed groups, where the relationships are still developing
- Extreme crises, like the death of a group member or a catastrophic loss

If the crisis is in the leader's personal life or family, they need you to be a pastor to them—a caring shepherd. It may be helpful for you to offer guidance to the group members, encouraging them to care for the leader. Whether it's a leader or a group member who's in need, remember:

- Hurting people value your presence over your words or skills. A call or visit can be very encouraging.
- Pray for and with people, asking God to restore their physical and spiritual health.

- Look for any ways you might serve them. Do they need help with household chores, family responsibilities, or food? Do they need help with transportation?

- Remember that shared pain is often the gateway to growth. This is often true not only for the individual but for the group as well.

- Know when to ask for help. Sometimes a particular need will be so large that it is beyond the ability of the group to meet it. Know where you or your leaders can turn for assistance in your church.

The natural tendency for most people is to withdraw from, not move toward people who are in pain. By your example, encourage leaders to come alongside people who are hurting. Guide them as they develop their heart of compassion.

Pain is the gift nobody wants.

—Philip Yancey

Time for a Checkup

It's time to reflect on your role as a guide for your leaders. Take a few minutes and consider the following questions.

1. How is your relationship with each of your leaders? Who do you know well? Not so well? Write out one or two questions you could ask that leader that would help you get to know him or her better.

2. How would your leaders rate you as a listener? What is one step you could take to improve your listening skills?

3. What are the growth edges for your leaders? Where do they need to grow spiritually? Where do they need to grow in their leadership skills?

4. Which small group leader is in a difficult season right now? What can you do to be a Barnabas for them?

Key Practice 3

Envisioning: Dream Together

Allow yourself to dream for a moment. When you think of a life-changing small group, what images come to mind?

- How do the people interact with each other?
- How do they care for one another? Serve one another? Encourage one another?
- In what ways are they meeting needs in the church and in the community at large?
- What would your church be like if every group functioned this way?

That's the basic concept behind vision. Any vision for community begins with a picture of what small groups would be like and how leaders would function in an ideal world.

Having a clear vision will affect your interaction with your leaders. It will impact your conversations with them, the resources you provide for them—it will even impact how you pray for them.

So when it comes to small groups, what's your vision? Take a moment and dream. Then write some of your thoughts below.

A vision expresses a desired future state that is better in some important way than what exists. It describes where you will be in the future and what it will be like.

—Paul Thornton, *Be the Leader*

Common Error

Most churches have a vision for the role small groups will play in their church. The vision often breaks down when it gets translated from a larger vision (what community looks like in the church as a whole) to the role each group and leader can play in helping the church reach that vision.

Coaches can easily fall into the trap of simply serving as a conduit for vision, parroting to group leaders the vision of the church. If that happens, the vision will not capture their hearts and there will be little connection to the day-to-day activities of small group leaders. Instead of simply casting vision to your leaders, create space for them to think about or dream about their group. Work with your leaders to create a clear and compelling vision for each of their groups—one that captures their heart and motivates them to action.

The Power of Vision

A vision has tremendous power when it is clear and compelling. It creates a hunger in us for something richer, fuller, or deeper than we are currently experiencing. It draws out our best thinking and energy.

Vision has the ability to:

Give Meaning. It helps leaders understand that group life is about more than leading a meeting; it's about life-change.

Create Hunger. It helps leaders grasp the bigger ideas of the mission of the church and the call to community. The gap between their skills and what's required to achieve the vision will create a hunger for training and coaching.

Change Focus. Vision can turn a leader's focus from themselves and their group members to the needs of those outside Christ and his community.

Give Hope. Leaders need hope; they need to know they can do this. God painted a vision for Abraham of a mighty nation coming through his bloodlines. "Against all hope, Abraham in hope believed" (Rom. 4:18). Vision inspired hope; hope enabled Abraham to believe and achieve the vision.

In *Organizing Genius*, Warren Bennis illustrates the power of vision with an account from one of the scientists who served on the Manhattan Project building the world's first nuclear bomb. The best and brightest engineers in the country were recruited to serve on the project.

They were assigned to work on the primitive computers of the period, doing energy calculations and other tedious jobs. But the army, obsessed with security, refused to tell them anything specific about the project. They didn't know that they were building a weapon that could end the war or even what their calculations meant. They were simply expected to do the work, which they did—slowly and not very well. Feynman, who supervised the technicians, prevailed on his superiors to tell the recruits what they were doing and why.

Permission was granted to lift the veil of secrecy, and Oppenheimer gave them a special lecture on the nature of the project and their own contribution.

"Complete transformation," Feynman recalled. "They began to invent ways of doing it better. They improved the scheme. They worked at night. They didn't need supervising in the night; they didn't need anything.

"They understood everything; they invented several of the programs that we used." Ever the scientist, Feynman calculated that the work was done "nearly ten times as fast" after it had meaning.

Crafting the Vision

Coaches can help leaders envision their roles in several key areas:

1. *Spiritual Growth.* Effective coaches model a life surrendered to Christ. The same is true for group leaders. Much of what leaders bring to group life is their own experience, maturity, and process for growth.

2. *Giftedness.* As trust develops, coaches are able to help leaders gain an accurate picture of their gifts and abilities. What are their strengths? Growth points? What is their God-given potential in leadership? What could God do through them and their group?

3. *Community.* Biblical community involves more than just small group meetings. Leaders will periodically need a fresh reminder of the purpose of

Good groups think they are on a mission from God.... They know going in that they will be expected to make sacrifices, but they know they are doing something worthy of their best selves.

—Warren Bennis,
Organizing Genius

community—transformation, connected relationships, compassion, and mission.

4. *The Leader's Role.* What is it that the church is asking of them? What is their unique place in helping the church achieve the overall vision?

5. *Ministry Multiplication.* Leaders seem to need constant encouragement and vision in this area. Leaders play a critical role in helping the church identify potential and future leaders, developing their skills and abilities (apprenticing), and multiplying the number of groups.

6. *Inclusivity.* All groups struggle at times with the challenges of adding new persons. Help leaders in your care regularly envision how to add new persons to their small groups at appropriate times and in appropriate ways.

Clarifying the Vision

It is important for coaches to help align each leader's vision for their group with the overall mission and vision for small groups in their church. For the most part, leaders do not look to their coach as the primary vision caster for the small groups ministry—the small groups pastor or director will often provide that vision. Instead, leaders look to their coach for help to clarify and personalize the vision.

To move from the general vision and values of your church's small group ministry to the specific vision for a group or a huddle, coaches rely on:

Prayer: Often viewed as a last resort, prayer should instead be the first place we turn for help in clarifying and personalizing vision. "If any of you lacks wisdom, you should ask God, who gives generously to all without finding fault, and it will be given to you" (James 1:5).

Examination: Look closely at the issues. Prayerfully consider the strengths of your leaders, the challenges ahead, and the opportunities for growth. Gain a clear picture of reality.

Experience: Think about your leaders and your past experiences with them. What have you faced in the past that can shed light on future opportunities?

Innovation: Try to imagine new ways to tackle the challenges ahead. "Wise men and women are always learning, always listening for fresh insights" (Prov. 18:15 MSG).

When completed, the vision should paint a picture for the leader of what they are trying to accomplish in their group and in the lives of group members.

Keep the Vision Alive

It is one thing for your small group leaders to understand the vision for community in your church, or the vision for how their small group can change and grow. But for leaders to own the vision with enthusiasm and to translate it into action requires coaches to continually re-cast the vision. Why?

As odd as it sounds, leaders have lives. While they may be passionate about their small group, they also have jobs, families, and other interests in life. Most are not thinking 24/7 about their small group. Life can crowd out the vision.

Paul encouraged Titus to "remind the people" of Crete—a prompting to all of us that vision "leaks." Unless you continually remind your leaders of the vision, you may find they are wandering aimlessly with no clear sense of purpose or direction.

Here are some ideas to keep the vision alive:

Speak with clarity. If you can't speak the vision clearly, then odds are you don't understand and own it completely yourself.

Speak with conviction. When you talk about the vision, make sure your language is compelling, focused, and balanced.

Utilize every opportunity to clarify, cast, and recast the vision. Huddles, training events, group visits, conversations, emails, and phone calls are all prime opportunities to share key vision components or to unpack an element of the vision. Be constantly on the watch for opportunities to creatively connect the vision to common activities. For example, a conversation in the church lobby with someone who is new to your church is a great chance to emphasize the hunger for community to a leader.

Use Scripture. The Bible is filled with passages on community and metaphors about doing life together in community. As you share with leaders, use these passages to support the vision for small groups.

Genesis 1:24–2:25	Mark 3:14
Genesis 6, 17	John 17
Exodus 18	Acts 2:41–47; 4:32–37
Psalm 133	Romans 12
Proverbs 15:22	1 Corinthians 12
Proverbs 18:24	Ephesians 2 and 4
Ecclesiastes 4:9–10	1 Peter 5:1–4

Help leaders understand and own the church's vision. Provide time, space, and a safe place for leaders to process and ask their questions. This can be easily done in one-on-one conversations and in huddles.

Dream about the group and the possibilities for growth and outreach. Create space for leaders to dream and pray about God's desire for their groups—what is God calling them to do or be as a small group?

Help leaders break the larger vision into smaller, more manageable steps. For example, one of the first steps toward group multiplication (birthing) is to identify an apprentice leader. Who in their group has the potential to be an apprentice?

Use stories that work. Watch for stories from leaders or groups that capture the heart of the vision in action in your church. Share these with leaders in huddles or in one-on-one conversations.

Celebrate when leaders achieve parts of the vision. Celebration communicates clearly that what they are doing matters.

Vision doesn't stick; it doesn't have natural adhesive. Instead, vision leaks.

—Andy Stanley,
Leadership

Time for a Checkup

It's time to reflect on how you envision your leaders. Take a few minutes and consider the following questions.

1. How clear is the vision for community in your own mind? Take a moment and write it out.

2. Often there is a gap between a coach's vision for community—how groups ought to function and how leaders ought to lead—and the reality of group life as they know it. What is the gap between vision and reality for you?

3. Where can you create the kind of settings that would allow your leaders to dream about community? When could you do this next?

4. What is one step you could take for your leaders to clarify or to recast the vision for community?

5. What can you celebrate? What steps have leaders taken or what goals have they achieved? When could you recognize this?

Key Practice 4

Equipping: Develop Skills

Most coaches enter into their role with a belief that equipping is their primary goal, to offer the skills and training small group leaders need to be more effective in leading their group. In most cases, coaches will have previously served as a small group leader. They will know both the joys and the frustrations of group life. So with good intentions and humble hearts, coaches share with group leaders from their own experiences. Yet they often become frustrated when leaders don't eagerly receive and treasure their gems of wisdom. Why the resistance?

Leaders do need to grow and improve their skills. But equipping is not the primary resource leaders need or want from a coach. In fact, many leaders will not be open to skill coaching until you have developed a relationship with them. Offered too soon, skill development can turn any contact in the coach-leader relationship toward a performance-based rather than a shepherding relationship.

Leaders want their coach to provide a model for a surrendered life, to shepherd their spiritual development, and to provide vision. When those pieces are in place, then leaders will be open to skill development with their coach.

By equipping your leaders with key leadership skills, you are helping them become more effective in meeting the real needs of their small group members. Remember Priscilla and Aquila in Acts 18:23–28 who were influential in equipping Apollos. Though Apollos was already eloquent, instructed in the Word, fervent in spirit, and able to teach, he needed more training from this couple to improve and develop. All leaders need to improve their skills, even leaders who are well equipped and seasoned in the Lord.

So as you shepherd and guide your leaders, try to discern their growth edges. What are their strengths and weaknesses as a leader? Make some personal notes along the way. These insights will prove valuable later. As the trust between you builds, leaders will begin to share struggles or challenges they are facing in their group. In that moment, they are signaling that they are open to helpful ideas that will better equip them for leadership.

A Common Error

While the relationship with your leaders is important, don't get stuck there. It is easy to make the mistake of turning the coach-leader relationship into nothing more than a deep friendship. Coaches can spend years with a leader only to realize that they have cared for their needs without developing their skills. They have forged a good friendship but have done little to improve the leader's ability. It's a delicate balance to maintain between shepherding and equipping.

Building a caring, nurturing relationship with your leaders is important. In fact, this shepherding relationship is foundational to all your work with them. When leaders have a vision, they create a picture of where their group could go and what they could become. When that vision takes root in their heart, leaders can begin to identify skills they will need to learn or improve upon in order to take steps toward achieving the vision. When a leader recognizes his leadership gap, it can serve as a strong internal motivator and create a hunger for learning.

Equipping Made Practical

Seldom will a coach utilize the classroom setting to provide skill training for their leaders. More often the equipping will happen in less formal settings, like one-on-one conversations. Through these times you will begin to understand the opportunities for growth for each leader. As leaders share experiences or struggles with you, watch for teachable moments. You can use a variety of tools to equip your leaders in this setting, including:

- Your past experience with the issue, either in group leadership or in coaching other leaders.
- Wisdom from other group leaders in your church who have dealt with the issue effectively.
- Upcoming classroom training at your church or other seminars and conferences.
- Books or articles that have helped you deal with the issue. These can include trusted sources like websites for small group ministries.
- Tapes or CDs of training on the topic. Many churches have developed a lending library for this purpose.

If a single topic or theme emerges consistently in conversations with your leaders, like difficulty in keeping group discussions on track, then you will want to use part of your next huddle time to provide skill training in this area.

Here are some guidelines for the ongoing equipping of your leaders:

Affirm their gifts and abilities. Every leader will have strengths and weaknesses. Make sure to affirm your leaders and encourage ongoing development of their talents. Offer a balance of building into their strengths and shoring up their weaknesses. Consider asking leaders to share from their strengths in a huddle or leadership gathering as a way to develop others.

Teach from their experiences. Every experience—good and bad—provides an opportunity to learn. Listen for common themes to emerge from the groups you coach. As leaders share with you, watch for specific examples that can serve as a learning experience for all your leaders.

Discern their growth edges. Over time you will begin to observe areas that are consistently challenging for a group leader. You may see unhealthy patterns developing in their personal walk or in the leadership of their group. Offer resources and tools to develop their skills and abilities in these areas.

Solve problems with them. Problem-solving requires listening and understanding. Work to identify alternate solutions and help leaders decide which would be best for their small group. You may need to consult with a staff member or small group point person before committing to a plan.

Utilize role plays. Role plays are especially effective in helping leaders learn interpersonal skills. They can be highly effective in teaching leaders skills like conflict resolution, active listening, and asking effective questions.

Learn together. You cannot know the answer to every issue or problem your leaders will encounter. So when you don't know, admit it! Work together with your leader to find the answer through the Bible, another leader, a fellow coach, a staff member, or some other resource.

There really is no learning without doing ... adults know that they learn best on the job, from experience, by trying things out.
—Roger Schank, http://www.edutrue.tripod.com/c-files/mistakes.html

Opportunities for Growth

The range of skills in which your leaders will need equipping is limitless. As a leader grows and as their group matures, the challenges and opportunities change. New skills may be required—or at least a new level of expertise in utilizing existing skills.

Focus on providing the tools that are needed most so that equipping doesn't become overwhelming to you or your leaders. Think through the list below and mark the ones that stand out for the leaders you coach.

Modeling a surrendered life	Shepherding members to growth
Adding new members	Leading your group to serve together
Listening skills	Creating a safe environment
Apprentice selection and development	Stages of group life
Using the Bible in groups	Conflict resolution
Dealing with difficult people	Planning life-changing meetings
Choosing good curriculum	Worship in groups
Asking good questions	Group multiplication
Group outreach and evangelism	How to create a covenant
How to establish core values	Fostering intimacy and transparency
Caring for people in crisis	Prayer in small groups
Helpful information on these topics can be found in *Leading Life-Changing Small Groups* by Bill Donahue.	

Pay attention to the needs of your leaders. Plan conversations and events carefully so they will benefit your leaders in the areas where growth is needed. Pay attention to the pace of your equipping, keeping leaders challenged but not overwhelmed. And always do this in the context of your shepherding relationship with them.

Time for a Checkup

It's time to reflect on how you equip your leaders. Take a few minutes and consider the following questions.

1. Carefully evaluate your relationship with each of your leaders. At what level is your relationship? Place an X in the boxes next to the leader's name to reflect which practices you currently employ with each leader. What observations or application can you make from this chart regarding next steps with each leader?

Leader	Model	Guide	Envision	Equip

2. In which coaching relationships have you neglected envisioning or equipping in favor of friendship? How can you begin to change that coaching relationship?

3. What methods or tools are you currently using to develop skills in your leaders?

4. Review the list of skills (see "Opportunities for Growth"). What skills do your leaders need at this time? What is one step you can take in the next thirty days to equip them?

Part Four

The Coach's Toolbox

Claude Waddell was a master carpenter. He plied his trade in the 1950s and '60s, before circular saws and power-nailers were used as widely as they are today. A look inside his toolbox revealed his favorite tools. A folding ruler with the edges worn smooth. Wood-handled chisels with razor-sharp blades. A hammer whose handle fit his hand perfectly, shaped by years of use. A brace and bit, a crosscut saw, a level, a square.

There were other tools in his box as well. Highly specialized tools, used infrequently but still of great importance. When they were needed, he wielded them with the same skill and precision. All these tools, both the common and the highly specialized, were ultimately used for the same purpose: to transform nails, wood, and plaster into houses. He used these tools to shape a vision and a plan into reality.

The same could be said of any person who daily works in a trade—a plumber, a landscaper, an architect, a machinist, or an engineer. Each of them has invested the time and energy to become skilled at using the tools of their trade, whether a wrench or a computer.

As we look inside the coach's toolbox, you'll discover a variety of tools available. Some you will use regularly. Some you will need rarely, if ever. Your success in transforming your vision for community and in developing the small group leaders in your care will depend on the level of skill and expertise you develop in using each of these tools.

So get to know them well. Invest the time to learn when and how to use them. These tools may feel awkward at first, like the first time you tried to drive a nail with a hammer. But over time you will gain the skill and expertise to use them well.

An Overview of Coaching

Understanding Your Role

As a coach, you are one of the most strategic people in the life-change process. While the sole responsibility for the success of the ministry does not rest on you alone, you play a vital part. Your role in nurturing and developing group leaders is critical to the health and vitality of the small group ministry in your church. You are on the front lines of the ministry and will have the most contact with the group leaders in your care.

There are three essential components to your role as a coach: nurturing the soul of group leaders, developing the skills of group leaders, and building a leadership team.

1. Nurture the Soul of Group Leaders

The natural temptation for new coaches is to view their role as a mid-level management position in the small group structure. If you were to take that mindset, you would focus on the numeric measures (Is our ministry growing?) and the skill proficiency of your leaders.

But what leaders most need and desire is a shepherd. They are looking for someone to nurture and guide them spiritually. Leaders need to be growing spiritually in order to lead the growth of their group members. Growing leaders can say, as Paul did, "Follow my example as I follow the example of Christ" (1 Cor. 11:1).

You will spend much of your time in coaching nurturing the soul of each leader in your care. As you pay attention to their spiritual growth, you will often find your leaders are more responsive to your guidance on group leadership matters.

First and foremost, think of the leaders in your care as sheep in your flock. In John 10:14 Jesus said, "I am the good shepherd; I know my sheep and my sheep know me." That's a good model to follow, so spend time with your leaders. Get to know their strengths and weaknesses. Learn to love them. Build into them and release them into life-giving ministry.

2. Develop the Skills of Group Leaders

Leading a small group is not rocket science. You can shape people with moldable hearts and teachable spirits into slightly above average group leaders. But who wants to be average? Who hungers for mediocrity?

What we want to be, and what we want to have in our ministry, is highly effective small group leaders. Leaders who truly "get it." Leaders who understand the vision and own it. Leaders who are a joy to coach. Leaders whose groups are growing spiritually and from whom stories of life-change seem to come on a weekly basis.

Here's the reality: effective leaders are developed over time. When the occasional gem of a leader drops into our laps, we are at that moment, quite simply the beneficiaries of someone else's efforts to develop their leadership skills.

Group leaders often start out as group members who catch a vision for leadership. Over time they are shaped into effective leaders through mentoring, training, trying, failing, and practicing. A key component of your role as a coach will be to develop the skills of each current and potential leader in your care.

3. Build a Leadership Team

Your leadership team consists of coaches, apprentice coaches, small group leaders, and their apprentices. You may identify other persons or roles that would be helpful to include on your team—an outreach coordinator, a ministry connector, a training specialist. As a team you will work together to build a biblically functioning community—one that brings about real and lasting life-change in group members.

The apostle Paul taught and modeled the team-building principle to his protégé Timothy. He gave him this directive: "Pass on what you heard from me—the whole congregation saying Amen!—to reliable leaders who are competent to teach others" (2 Tim. 2:2 MSG). Here, Paul was describing four generations of leaders!

Paul was a team builder. Look at the teams of people who worked with him to build the church in Rome. Paul listed them in Romans 16: "Greet Priscilla and Aquila, my fellow workers ... Greet Andronicus and Junias, my relatives ... Greet Tryphena and Tryphosa, those women who work hard in the Lord ... Greet Asyncritus, Phlegon, Hermes, Patrobas, Hermas and the brothers with them" (NIV).

You probably will not name many of your children after these people, but they formed the foundational ministry teams for the church at Rome, a church that needed the strength of teams to survive ministry in the face of great difficulties.

An Overview of the Tools

There are three primary tools you will use as you build into your leaders. Remember, ultimately the work of a coach with leaders is twofold: to nurture the soul and to develop the skill of a group leader. Each of these tools has a unique role to play in that balance of nurture and development. How to best utilize each tool will be explained in greater detail later. For now, here's an overview:

> **One-on-One Conversations.** This tool is more about nurture than skill development, especially early on in your relationship with leaders. These conversations provide a face-to-face opportunity to understand and meet the unique needs of each leader in a way that you cannot in huddles or group visits, whether those needs are about spiritual growth or are an issue of group leadership.
>
> **Leadership Gatherings (Huddles).** Huddles provide the best opportunity to give both nurture and skill training to your leaders. They also offer the opportunity to model community. While you might choose to emphasize skill over nurture in a particular meeting, over the course of a year there should be a balance in your huddles.

Group Visits. Visits allow you to observe firsthand the leadership skills and growth edges for your leaders. They also allow you the chance to affirm your leader in the presence of the group. In general, group visits are more about developing skills than nurturing the soul.

If we were to chart out the purpose of each of these tools, it would look like this:

	Nurture		Develop Skill
One-on-Ones			
Leadership Huddles			
Group Visits			

Where Should I Begin?

If you are new to the coaching role, it is always best to begin by building a relationship with each of your leaders. This is done best in a one-on-one setting. This coaching tool is the least intimidating to the leader. Depending on your personality type, you may also find this tool is the one you are most comfortable using to nurture and develop your leaders.

After you have built a relationship, it is then time to visit the leader's group. Finally, introduce your leaders to the huddle concept. Invest the majority of the huddle time in the first few meetings to relationship building.

If you are an experienced coach and a new leader is added to your existing huddle, try to meet with that leader one-on-one as soon as possible. Knowing their coach will make it easier for the leader to engage in existing relationships within your huddle. A visit to their small group can come later, after the relationship is established.

One-on-One Conversations

Imagine a conversation with a shepherd about the individual sheep in his flock. They may all look the same to you, but each of his sheep has unique needs and habits.

"See that one over there, the one with the ragged ear? It has a firm conviction that the grass *outside* the fence is better than the grass inside. So day after day, he pushes his head through the barbed wire fence to nibble on forbidden delicacies. And when he pulls his head back through the fence, he snags that right ear.

"See that lamb, the one struggling to walk? Her mother accidentally stepped on her when she was young. Broke her leg. Ewes are generally good mothers, but occasionally these things happen. The lamb is healing fine, but she'll walk with a limp the rest of her life."

Like a good shepherd, coaches know the leaders in their care. As you meet one-on-one with your leaders, you will learn more about their personal walk with Christ, their family life, and their deepest needs. You'll gain insights into the uniqueness of each leader—their strengths and weaknesses. These insights will help you nurture and develop your leaders. Nothing can substitute for personal time with them.

Relationships First

An easy assumption for any coach would be that the purpose of one-on-one meetings is to manage the small group ministry—to use the face-to-face time to make sure the leaders are doing the right things. What curriculum are they using? Is life-change happening in their small group? Are they adding new people? Are they developing their apprentice?

These are important questions and they often surface in these meetings. But the primary purpose of a one-on-one meeting is for the coach to establish a personal, pastoral relationship with the leader. This personal touch assures the leaders that they are valued. It affirms both the leader and their ministry. When done well, leaders feel empowered and supported by their coach and the church.

A personal connection is what leaders most desire from coaches. As you prepare to meet with a group leader, keep these goals in mind:

Build and grow your relationship. This personal connection is the foundation of all your work with your leaders. Ask questions and listen deeply so you get to know each of your leaders well.

Guide their spiritual growth. Get to know their story. How did they come to Christ? To your church? Use the Shepherding Plan (see page 65) to help them determine what their next steps of spiritual growth might be.

Problem solve issues in group life. Group life can be messy. Your one-on-one times can provide a safe place for leaders to discuss their leadership struggles.

Envision your leaders. Group leaders will primarily catch the vision for community from the point leader of your small group ministry and through communication from the main platform. Utilize your one-on-one time to re-emphasize and re-cast that vision, stressing the portions that impact their group and their leadership.

Guidelines for Effective One-on-One Conversations

Build strong, healthy relationships with your leaders by following these basic principles:

Focus on Nurture More Than Skill Development

The primary purpose in one-on-one meetings is to nurture the soul of your leader, not to increase their effectiveness in leadership or to develop their leadership abilities. A recent survey at our church emphasized this need—leaders want their coach to be a shepherd first.

As the trust grows in your relationship, the leader will begin to share with you at a more personal level. Be patient; this may take time. They will open up about personal struggles or leadership challenges—issues they would not have shared with you at first. They may invite your input into struggles they are having as they lead their group.

The depth of your relationship and the impact of your one-on-ones will increase over time if you follow these principles:

> **Listen intently.** "Everyone should be quick to listen, slow to speak and slow to become angry" (James 1:19).
>
> **Strive for authenticity and openness through honest communication.** "Instead, speaking the truth in love, we will in all things grow up into him who is the Head, that is, Christ" (Eph. 4:15).
>
> **Help them determine their next steps of growth.** "And we pray this in order that you may live a life worthy of the Lord and may please him in every way: bearing fruit in every good work, growing in the knowledge of God" (Col. 1:10).

Focus on Spiritual Concerns More Than Organizational Issues

Ministry growth strategies, reporting, and organizational charts should be saved for huddles and planning meetings. In one-on-one meetings, leaders rely on their coach primarily for guidance and help with spiritual and personal issues.

Leaders are looking to their coaches to be a caring, loving shepherd, not a spiritual director. Ask questions about their walk with Christ, their personal spiritual disciplines, and their participation in the life of the church. Pray for them and with them. (For help on this, see "Guiding Spiritual Growth: Developing a Shepherding Plan" on page 64.)

As you work to increase the spiritual depth of your leaders, the quality of their leadership will improve.

Focus on Encouragement More Than Management

Many leaders are apprehensive, even anxious, before their first meeting with a coach. They fear the meetings will be less like a conversation with a friend and more like a trip to the vice principal's office. Communicate clearly to them before the meeting, and again as it begins, that you hope the time will be encouraging to them.

The apostle Paul's ministry provides a great example for coaches in the one-on-one meeting. He summarizes his ministry to the church in Thessalonica in this way: "With each of you we were like a father with his child, holding your hand, whispering encouragement, showing you step-by-step how to live well before God, who called us into his own kingdom, into this delightful life" (1 Thess. 2:11–12 MSG).

Other passages show just how important this ministry of personal encouragement was to Paul:

> *Acts 16:40*: After being released from jail, Paul and Silas went to Lydia's house and encouraged the people meeting there.
>
> *Acts 20:1*: After an uproar in Ephesus, Paul called the disciples together and encouraged them.
>
> *Acts 20:2*: On his way from Ephesus to Greece, Paul stopped in churches and towns along the way and encouraged Christians.
>
> *Colossians 4:8*: Paul sent Tychicus to the church at Colosse to encourage them.

What leaders need most from their coach is to feel supported and encouraged, not *managed*. Help your leaders along in their spiritual walk with encouraging words. A good rule of thumb is a 5:1 ratio of encouragement to criticism, even if the criticism is constructive.

Focus on Frequent Connection More Than High-Impact Conversations

Schedule a regular meeting and make it a part of your ministry in your leaders' lives. The more frequent your meetings, the more quickly your relationship will deepen. Create a Care Covenant (see page 121) to help you determine the frequency of your meetings. In addition to one-on-one meetings, contact each of your leaders regularly. Utilize phone calls, emails, and hallway conversations at church to stay in touch.

How often you meet with a leader will depend upon their needs and your availability. New leaders or leaders of groups in crisis will require more of your time. This may mean several contacts during a week in order to help a leader navigate a conflict or to help a new leader through their first few small group meetings.

How Do I Do This?

Here are four simple steps to planning and leading a one-on-one conversation.

1. Pray

This step is easily overlooked. Spend time praying for and with each of your leaders. Paul said he prayed often and with great intensity for his leaders. In Philippians 1:3–11, Paul thanks God for his leaders in Philippi and for God's continued work in their lives. He prayed that God would give him the chance to be with them again, and he prayed for their personal walk, that their love for Christ might abound and that they might experience the fullness of Christ's righteousness.

Before your one-on-one meeting, pray that God will lead and guide the conversation. Ask him to show you areas where your leaders need to be affirmed as well as those where they may need to be challenged.

2. Prepare

Prepare for your meetings, considering your conversation's focus and purpose in advance. Good preparation will maximize your time together. Think through the following questions as you prepare:

1. What is your sense of how this leader is doing spiritually?
2. What are the one or two main issues you would like to discuss when you meet?
3. What issues need follow-up from previous one-on-one meetings?
4. Is there any item, a reason to offer praise, or a concern, that you need to discuss from your last group visit or huddle?

3. Personalize

As you meet with your leaders, keep the time personal. Each leader needs individual attention and care. Listen carefully to your leaders and offer feedback to them based on your observations. Help them evaluate their life and leadership so they will celebrate their strengths and continue to grow in their areas of weakness. Remember to speak the truth in love.

Be flexible enough to respond to any issues they are facing before moving to your agenda for the time together. There will always be time to cover the most essential agenda items—don't worry if you don't accomplish all your goals for every meeting. It is more important to deal with the conflict that happened in Sarah's group last week than to cast vision for her to find an apprentice. Better to listen and understand the family crisis that Bob is facing—to shepherd Bob—than to try to offer suggestions for improving the discussion level in his group meetings.

Work with your leaders to discover their strengths and their growth edges, primarily in their spiritual life but also in their leadership. Affirm their unique gifts and talents.

Partner with your leaders in their overall development. Look for one or two practical things you can do to help them grow. Exchange ideas, key Bible verses, illustrations, and personal experiences that might help them toward their goals. Together determine specific action steps they can work on before your next meeting (a book to read, a spiritual discipline to practice, a relationship to build, etc.).

4. Perspective

After each meeting (or series of meetings) gain insight and perspective by evaluating the time spent with your leaders. Ask yourself a series of questions:

1. Did my leader feel heard?
2. Did my leader feel cared for and supported?
3. Did I serve them in a tangible way?
4. Was the balance between nurture and development appropriate?
5. What issues need follow-up before our next meeting?
6. Did I capitalize on teachable moments in their life?
7. What was one thing they felt challenged by or wanted to know more about?

Helpful Questions

The primary goal of one-on-one time with your leaders is shepherding—to assist them in their spiritual growth. Your meetings will also provide you with opportunities to personally coach leaders in skill development and team building. Many of these opportunities will come through their questions and through challenges of leading their small group. Think through the purpose of your next one-on-one meeting. Choose or adapt questions from the list below to help start the conversation with your leader. Three or four questions are often enough to fill an hour of conversation.

Nurture the Soul
Spiritual Life Questions

When did you become a Christian?

What person was most influential in your decision?

How did you come to be a part of this church?

Do you have any lingering concerns or issues about this church?

Where have you served in the church? How did those experiences impact you?

What spiritual disciplines do you practice regularly?

What spiritual disciplines would you like to add or learn?

In what areas of your life do you struggle with the temptation to sin?

Relationship-Building Questions

What people have been influential in your life? How?

What books have impacted your life? How?

What have been the major turning points in your life?

What communicates love to you?

What is your personality or temperament?

What makes you sad? Brings you joy?

What do you dream about?

What are your fears?

What personal issues do you need assistance with?

Develop the Skills

Although skill development is not the primary focus of one-on-one meetings, the meetings can offer the leader some freedom to admit struggles they might not express in a more public setting. Try to include at least one question from this area in each one-on-one.

> What two things are going well in your group right now?
>
> Where are you seeing life-change happen in your group?
>
> If you had a magic wand, what one issue or concern in your group would you resolve immediately?
>
> How are you developing your members spiritually?
>
> What issues or problems are you currently facing in your small group? How can I help you with these?
>
> What do you consider to be strengths in your leadership?
>
> Which skills would you most like to grow in?

Build the Team

> How are you casting vision for leadership to your group members?
>
> Who are you pouring your life into as an apprentice leader?
>
> In what ways are you shepherding and developing your apprentice leader(s)?
>
> What resources or tools do you need to assist you in this?
>
> As your group increases in size, in what ways are you preparing the group to eventually birth (multiply)?

Sharpen Your Skills

Studies have proven that it takes seven to twenty-one repetitions to learn a new task and another seven to twenty-one before that new task becomes a comfortable habit. Very few coaches are instantly comfortable in leading a one-on-one meeting. So give yourself grace and time to learn. Here are some tips to help you continually improve your one-on-one skills.

Model

Your leaders will look at your life as the standard. If you are not growing spiritually, then it will be difficult to motivate your leaders to grow. So do your best to model a Christ-filled life for them. Model vulnerability, honesty, and authenticity in your one-on-one times. If it is helpful, share examples or stories from your walk with Christ and your group leadership that illustrate your personal growth. (For more information on modeling, see "A Coach's Key Practices" on page 29.)

Observe

Study your leaders. Learn as much as possible about their talents, skills, motivation, energy, interests, and spiritual growth. Try to be with them in as many different contexts and settings as possible. Your observations can trigger helpful topics for your one-on-one conversations.

Also try to observe other coaches in one-on-one settings. Spending time with an experienced, seasoned coach will allow you to learn from their leadership.

Seek Feedback

Periodically ask your leaders for honest feedback on your coaching relationship with them. Do they feel supported, encouraged, and resourced to lead their group? How would they like to see their relationship with you improve? Do your best to listen without becoming defensive. Even constructive criticism can be difficult to hear. Thank them for their input and commit it to thought and prayer.

Inspire

Coaches don't control their players; they inspire them with words of motivation and affirmation. Help your leaders see their full potential. Name the skills, talents, and abilities that you see in your leaders which they may not see. Dream with them about the possibilities of what God might do in them and through them. Cheer them on!

Train

Help your leaders reach their full potential. Provide them with the best training, tools, and techniques so they can lead effectively. Good training will change how they lead and will impact the life and health of their group. Watch for new books, tapes, or training seminars that would be helpful to you and your leaders.

Men and Women in Coaching Relationships

Coaches serve under the authority of their local church leadership. Whether or not it is appropriate for men and women to be involved in a coach/leader relationship will most likely be determined by the elders or the governing body of your church.

Coaches should also be mindful of the context in which they serve, considering the culture of their church and the surrounding community. Some cultures would view it as inappropriate for an unmarried man and woman to meet together. To do so in this context could potentially damage the reputation of the leader or of the church in your community.

If you do coach leaders of the opposite gender, the following statement from the elders at Willow Creek can serve as a helpful guideline: "Pursue the kind of purity and loyalty in relationships that led New Testament writers to describe them in terms of family: brothers and sisters. 'Do not rebuke an older man harshly, but exhort him as if he were your father. Treat younger men as brothers, older women as mothers, and younger women as sisters, with absolute purity' (1 Tim. 5:1–2)."

Three Tests for Relational Purity

It is important to constantly examine the thoughts and attitudes of your heart (Heb. 4:12) in order to maintain relational purity. Asking another coach, a spouse, or a staff member to serve as an accountability partner is also helpful. Regularly share your schedule with them and give them permission to ask questions about anything that appears inappropriate.

Before scheduling or conducting a meeting with a person of the opposite sex, ask yourself these questions:

1. Is there anything impure about my thoughts or intentions in regard to this other person?
2. Would I change my actions or my relating patterns toward this individual if another person were present at the meeting, like my spouse or a trusted friend?
3. Would I change my behavior or relating patterns with this individual if the content of our conversation were to be shared publicly at our next worship service?

If the answer to any of these questions is yes, then you should do one or more of the following:

- Postpone or cancel your meeting with the leader.
- Seek out wise counsel and accountability from a friend, spouse, or staff member.
- Ask your small group point person to find a new coach for this leader.

▶ Development Aid ▶

Guiding Spiritual Growth
Developing a Shepherding Plan

This shepherding plan is based on Willow Creek's Five G developmental framework—Grace, Growth, Group, Gifts, and Good Stewardship. It can be used as a guide to discussing spiritual growth with a leader. This framework may not fit your church's strategy or language, so feel free to adapt it to fit your setting. The framework you use is not important; having a framework to utilize is!

Three key words to remember in using this plan are:

Assessment. Provide a copy of the plan for your leaders a week or so before your next one-on-one. Ask them to spend some time thinking and praying about each of the areas. What is your perception of how you are doing in these areas? Some leaders will prefer to journal their thoughts, while others will make a few notes in the boxes.

Advancement. Leaders should consider what next steps of growth God might be asking them to take in each area of their walk with Christ. List as many steps as possible, then bring the list and the above assessment to their next one-on-one meeting with you.

Accountability. When you meet, ask the leader to share their assessment and steps for advancement. Listen intently—this may be the most vulnerable place in your relationship with the leader. Ask clarifying questions along the way. Encourage and gently challenge the leader as they share.

After hearing all the possible next steps, help the leader choose one they would be willing to take in the coming weeks. How will they begin? What will success look like in this area of their life?

Ask permission to follow up and see how they are progressing, perhaps at your next one-on-one, via email, or by a phone call.

▶

Shepherding Plan

	Questions	My Plan
Grace To experience and extend saving grace (2 Cor. 5:18–19).	• How is my relationship with the Father? • Am I living empowered by the Holy Spirit? • With what lost person am I building a relationship? • Am I inviting new persons to the weekend services?	
Growth To grow in having Christ spiritually formed in us (Heb. 10:24–25).	• Am I reading and applying God's Word to my life? • Am I regularly spending quiet times alone with God? • Does God have consistent control over my mind, heart, and body?	
Group To shepherd one another in loving, authentic community (Gal. 6:2).	• Do I have strong relationships in my life? • Am I a good listener? • Do I have healthy relational boundaries? • Do I respect the boundaries of others? • How am I doing at speaking the truth in love?	
Gifts To discover, develop, and deploy our spiritual gifts to serve the body of Christ (Rom. 12:6–8).	• Am I serving in my area of passion and giftedness? • Do I consistently approach the use of my gifts with a servant's heart? • Is there a sense of joy around my serving?	
Good Stewardship To steward our time and treasures for God's redemptive purposes (Matt. 25:40).	• Is there balance in my use of my time? • Am I using my financial resources in a God-honoring way? • How am I doing at reaching out beyond the walls of my church?	

Adapted from *Leading Life-Changing Small Groups* (Zondervan, 1996).

▶Development Aid▶

Guiding Skill Development
Eight Guides for Conversations between a Coach and a Leader

As you begin meeting one-on-one with a leader, your first steps will be to build a relationship and to establish a Care Covenant (see pages 121–22). You will want to learn about their relational world (including family, friends, and work), their spiritual journey, and their leadership experience.

Over time your conversations will begin to include elements of skill development for the leaders. The following Coaching Conversation Guides will plan for these talks. They focus on eight practices that are key to the success of small group leaders:

Modeling Personal Growth

Shepherding Your Leaders

Building Authentic Relationships

Resolving Conflict in a Healthy Manner

Extending Care and Compassion

Becoming an Inclusive Community

Reaching Out to Seekers

Developing Future Leaders

Here are some guidelines for effective use of these conversations:

1. Always begin by checking in—how is the leader doing personally? How is their group doing? Skill training should take place only if their heart and head can receive it.

2. There are four main sections to each guide, and they correspond to the four key practices of coaching. The sections are :

   a. Model—designed to help coaches prepare their heart and their thoughts for the one-on-one conversation.

   b. Guide—questions to help assess progress the leader is making in this skill or areas where they might need assistance.

   c. Envision—information and questions to help leaders catch the purpose and value of this particular skill.

   d. Equip—additional training resources for the coach and/or leader.

3. As you review the conversation guides, choose the sections and questions that will be most helpful for the leader. Each guide contains enough questions for several meetings, so prayerfully consider which questions are best for this leader at this time. One or two well-worded questions will be enough for a one hour conversation with most leaders.*

---

*Note: Special thanks to Mike Hurt, from McLean Bible Church. His Coaching Conversations were immensely helpful in shaping these guides. Portions of those conversations are used here with his permission and the full text can be seen at www.smallgroupresources.org.

Coaching Conversation 1: Modeling Personal Growth

The Big Idea

To help leaders follow God with increasing joy, humility, and gratitude so they are growing in the life of full devotion they are inviting others to lead.

Key Verses

Follow my example as I follow the example of Christ. —1 Corinthians 11:1

Not that I have already obtained all this, or have already been made perfect, but I press on to take hold of that for which Christ Jesus took hold of me. —Philippians 3:12 NIV

I consider everything a loss because of the surpassing worth of knowing Christ Jesus my Lord, for whose sake I have lost all things. I consider them garbage, that I may gain Christ. —Philippians 3:8

Model (for the Coach)

As you prepare for this conversation, consider the following:

What do you do to abide in Christ daily?

What are some things that pull you away from Christ?

Which of your experiences might help your leaders grow?

Guide

Invite the leader to share their spiritual journey with you. Listen intently and watch for key points of growth or struggle in their journey.

What spiritual disciplines or practices have been helpful in your growth to this point?

Which disciplines are you able to practice on a regular basis?

Who are three people who have influenced your spiritual journey? How did they influence you?

What books or authors have helped shape your walk with Christ?

What issues or sins seem to be a recurring theme in your journey? How do you deal with these temptations?

Envision

Pressing on is a lifelong process. Paul challenges us to have the same attitude as his in Philippians 3:15. Pressing on is not always easy, but we must not give up. Persevering does not only mean facing obstacles; it also speaks of consistency, persistence, and a life of learning. To press on, we must learn how to continue growing in all stages of life. Each of us faces similar situations in our faith journey.

We face exciting times of growth and God's activity. We wish all our times were like these. However, we need to be careful that we don't get spiritually lazy during these times.

• When did you last experience a time of growth in your spiritual life?

We face times of suffering and faith challenges. These are times we wish we could avoid. While these times are tough to live through, they are fertile ground for spiritual growth. The key to continued growth during these times is to search for God's hand and purpose in the suffering or faith challenges.

• When is the last time you experienced a time of suffering or faith challenges?

• What helped you to see God's hand through your struggles?

We face times of feeling distant from God. In the midst of these times, we long for God's activity in our lives. The key to continued growth during these times is to pursue God even if it seems he can't be found. Changing your routine can help refresh your walk with God.

- When was the last time you felt distant from God?
- What did you do to restore the closeness?

Equip

Disciplines such as prayer, Bible study, worship, giving, solitude, accountability, and others can all help you to pursue God.

- What habits or disciplines would you like to develop to help in your walk with Christ? How can I assist you in this?

Resources you can recommend:

The Life You've Always Wanted by John Ortberg is a good life application study.

Celebration of Discipline by Richard Foster is a classic study in the spiritual disciplines.

Coaching Conversation 2: Shepherding Your Leaders

The Big Idea

To help leaders listen and intentionally explore the work of God in group members, in order to help them identify and take next steps of spiritual growth.

Key Verses

Their responsibility is to equip God's people to do his work and build up the church, the body of Christ, until we come to such unity in our faith and knowledge of God's Son that we will be mature and full grown in the Lord, measuring up to the full stature of Christ.   —Ephesians 4:12–13 NLT

And we pray this in order that you may live a life worthy of the Lord and may please him in every way: bearing fruit in every good work, growing in the knowledge of God.   —Colossians 1:10 NIV

Grow in the grace and knowledge of our Lord and Savior Jesus Christ.   —2 Peter 3:18

Model (for the Coach)

As you prepare for this conversation, consider the following:

In what ways have you provided an example of a shepherd to this leader?

How can you better utilize your one-on-one times to shepherd the leader in their growth?

Guide

Take a moment of quiet meditation and reflect on your own small group leadership. What components of shepherding are natural for you to do with your flock? What components require intention and work? Depending on your gifts and experience, shepherding may be challenging for you as a leader. The questions below will help you.

What steps have you taken to learn the spiritual journey of each of your group members?

What signs are you seeing that would indicate group members are growing spiritually?

Where are group members in their spiritual journey? What issues are they struggling with?

How are you encouraging the work that God is doing in your group members?

What steps are you taking to lead group members to growth? (Encourage leaders to think of ways to help members grow in the time between meetings as well as in formal meeting times.)

Envision

For a fresh understanding of the shepherding heart of God, encourage your leaders to review these key passages. You may want to read and discuss them together.

Psalm 23   John 10:1–21   1 Peter 5:1–4
Ezekiel 34   John 21:15–19

- What do you learn about God's heart for shepherding in these passages?
- What areas of shepherding come naturally to you? Which ones do you need to work to develop?

Equip

Resources that can help your leaders grow in this area include:

"Making Disciples" in *Leading Life-Changing Small Groups* (pp. 147–50).

"Asking Good Questions" in *Leading Life-Changing Small Groups* (pp. 114–18).

How People Grow by Henry Cloud and John Townsend.

Coaching Conversation 3: Building Authentic Relationships

The Big Idea

To help leaders maximize interaction in both formal and informal gatherings so that group members build authentic relationships in an environment of mutual accountability.

Key Verses

As iron sharpens iron, a friend sharpens a friend.

—Proverbs 27:17 NLT

The whole point of what we're urging is simply *love*—love uncontaminated by self-interest and counterfeit faith—a life open to God.

—1 Timothy 1:5 MSG

Be devoted to one another in brotherly love. Honor one another above yourselves.

—Romans 12:10 NIV

Let the word of Christ dwell in you richly as you teach and admonish one another with all wisdom, and as you sing psalms, hymns and spiritual songs with gratitude in your hearts to God.

—Colossians 3:16 NIV

Therefore encourage one another and build each other up, just as in fact you are doing.

—1 Thessalonians 5:11 NIV

And let us consider how we may spur one another on toward love and good deeds.

—Hebrews 10:24 NIV

Model (for the Coach)

As you prepare for this conversation, consider the following:

How do you model openness and authenticity in one-on-ones with this leader?

What activities or practices do you use to encourage authentic relationships in your leadership gatherings?

Are there any behaviors you need to change (judging, criticizing, belittling, minimizing, inappropriate humor, etc.) to foster a deeper relationship with this leader?

Guide

Relationship building happens during the meeting time as well as between meetings. As you talk with leaders, help them think of ways to make the most of both opportunities.

During the Meeting

How long have group members been together? How have they bonded?
How would you describe the discussion and interaction in a typical meeting?
How do you deal with people who may talk too little, too much, or too long?
How would you like to see the discussions change or improve?

Between Meetings

How do you stay in contact with group members between meetings?
How do group members connect with one another in the time between meetings (phone, email, coffee or meals together, trips, etc.)?
What group activities, events, or retreats has the leader planned in addition to regular study or meeting times?

Envision

If it would be helpful, offer examples of how other leaders have used the time between meetings to build relationships with and between group members.

Leaders can sometimes deepen the sharing and interaction in a group meeting by changing the type of curriculum that is used. Offer these simple ideas to help your leaders.

Guidelines for Choosing a Good Study

Doctrinal Purity: Studies should be Christ-centered. Avoid topics that will polarize people within the group.

Relational in Nature: Every study must have a personal, sharing component.

Application Oriented: The goal is action and accountability, not just knowledge.

Sensitivity to Needs: Keep in mind the length of the group meeting, the amount of homework group members are willing to do, and their spiritual maturity.

Reflect on the following thoughts with your leader:

Community life is the place where our limitations, our fears and our egoism are revealed to us. We discover our poverty and our weaknesses, our inability to get along with some people, our mental and emotional blocks, our affective or sexual disturbances, our seemingly insatiable desires, our frustrations and jealousies, our hatred and our wish to destroy. While we are alone, we could believe we loved everyone. Now that we are with others, living with them all the time, we realize how incapable we are of loving, how much we deny to others, how closed in on ourselves we are … Community is the place where the power of the ego is revealed and where it is called to die so that people become one body and give much life. —Jean Vanier, *Community and Growth*

Equip

Resources that can help your leaders grow in this area include the following sections from *Leading Life-Changing Small Groups*:

"Choosing and Using the Right Curriculum" (pp. 101–3)

"Asking Good Questions" (pp. 114–16)

"Relationship Building Exercises" (pp. 126–32)

Coaching Conversation 4:
Resolving Conflict in a Healthy Manner
The Big Idea

To help leaders create an environment where the truth is spoken in love so group members experience reconciliation in their relationships with God and with other people.

Key Verses

Finally, all of you, live in harmony with one another; be sympathetic, love as brothers, be compassionate and humble. Do not repay evil with evil or insult with insult, but with blessing, because to this you were called so that you may inherit a blessing.   —1 Peter 3:8 NIV

Patiently correct, rebuke, and encourage your people with good teaching.   —2 Timothy 4:2 NLT

Bear with each other and forgive one another if any of you has a grievance against someone. Forgive as the Lord forgave you.   —Colossians 3:13

If a brother or sister sins, go and point out the fault, just between the two of you. If they listen to you, you have won them over.   —Matthew 18:15

Model (for the Coach)

As you prepare for this conversation, consider the following:

What is your pattern for dealing with conflict in your own life?

What would you consider to be your strengths and weaknesses in this area?

Is there any lingering or unresolved conflict or tension between you and this leader? What is your plan to resolve it?

Guide

Ephesians 4:15 commands us to "speak the truth in love." Which part of that is harder for you—speaking the truth or speaking in love? How does this impact your ability to engage in healthy conflict resolution?

What do you understand to be the teaching from Scripture on how we are to resolve conflict in relationships?

In your own life, what is your natural pattern for conflict resolution? How does this line up with or differ from the teaching of Scripture?

In what ways have you dealt with disagreements, hurt feelings, or broken relationships in your group?

What tension or conflicts, if any, exist between members of your group right now?

Envision

Help your leaders understand that conflict is normal and natural in group life. It will happen even in the best groups. As Larry Crabb says, "Conflict is latent in every human relationship at every moment. It simply awaits a trigger to get it going."

Help leaders understand some of the root causes of conflict in group life.

Group Stages: In the early days of a small group, everyone thinks they love each other—because they really don't know each other. But after a few meetings the new begins to wear off. We

▶

start to see each other's wounds and washouts. Within six months or so, it's not uncommon for groups to experience their first conflict.

Relationally Unaware Group Members: A relationally unaware person seems to either be clueless or uncaring about interpersonal or group dynamics.

Needy Group Members: This is someone, who for very legitimate reasons, needs a little extra love and attention from the group. Tension can come when these needs are chronic or long-term.

Interpersonal Tension: Sometimes people just rub each other the wrong way and everyone can sense it. Usually the person involved is not trying to offend or be a pain. Sometimes personalities clash and friction develops between group members.

Study together to better know the biblical view on conflict resolution. In addition to those listed above, these passages provide helpful guidelines for leaders:

Matthew 18:15–17

Ephesians 4:26–27

Proverbs 15:23, 28

2 Timothy 2:24

Matthew 5:23–24

1 Corinthians 13

Proverbs 20:3

James 4:2

Equip

Resources that can help your leaders grow in this area include:

"Conflict Management" in *Leading Life-Changing Small Groups* (pp. 122–24)

"Care-fronting: The Creative Way through Conflict" in *Leading Life-Changing Small Groups* (pp. 125–26)

"How to Have a Good Fight" in *Walking the Small Group Tightrope* by Bill Donahue and Russ Robinson

Caring Enough to Confront by David Augsberger

Coaching Conversation 5: Extending Care and Compassion

The Big Idea

To help leaders and groups offer tangible expressions of Christ's compassion as they care for people's needs personally and through the resources of the church.

Key Verses

If we don't love people we can see, how can we love God, whom we have not seen? And God himself has commanded that we must love not only him but our Christian brothers and sisters, too.

—1 John 4:20–21 NLT

Serve one another in love.

—Galatians 5:13 NLT

Carry each other's burdens.

—Galatians 6:2

Love one another deeply, from the heart.

—1 Peter 1:22

Each of you should use whatever gift you have received to serve others, as faithful stewards of God's grace in its various forms.

—1 Peter 4:10

Model (for the Coach)

As you prepare for this conversation, consider the following:

In what ways have you extended care and compassion to your leaders?

How might the leader need you to extend care or compassion in this conversation?

What are some of the obstacles to caring for this leader? How can you overcome them?

Guide

How does your group care for one another as the body of Christ? (Invite the leader to share some recent examples. Watch for indications that the leader is encouraging the group to care for each other, in addition to personally caring for group members.)

If your group struggles in this area, how might you guide them to more tangible expressions of Christ's compassion?

How does the group balance Galatians 6:2 (carry each other's burdens) with Galatians 6:5 (each of you should carry your own load)?

What needs exist in the group that may be beyond their ability to meet?

Envision

Spend time with your leaders reflecting on the following quotes from Scripture and Christian authors.

In this world you will have trouble.

—Jesus, John 16:33

Praise be to the God and Father of our Lord Jesus Christ, the Father of compassion and the God of all comfort, who comforts us in all our troubles, so that we can comfort those in any trouble with the comfort we ourselves receive from God.

—Paul, 2 Corinthians 1:3–4

When life kicks us in the stomach, we want someone to be with us as we are, not as he or she wishes us to be. We don't want someone trying to make us feel better. That effort, no matter how well intended, creates a pressure that adds to our distress.

—Larry Crabb, *Shattered Dreams*

▶

I feel helpless around people in pain. Helpless and guilty. I stand beside them, watching facial features contort and listening to their sighs and moans, deeply aware of the huge gulf between us. I cannot penetrate their suffering, I can only watch. Whatever I attempt to say seems weak and stiff, as if I'd memorized the lines for a school play. —Philip Yancey, *Where Is God When It Hurts?*

- How do these thoughts reflect your own feelings or experiences?
- In what ways have you seen this to be true for yourself or members of your group?

Equip

Resources that can help your leaders grow in this area include:

List of resources in the church or the community where leaders can go for assistance

"Providing Care" in *Leading Life-Changing Small Groups* (pp. 153–56)

Where is God When It Hurts by Philip Yancey

Shattered Dreams by Larry Crabb

"Treating Wounds or Training Soldiers" in *Walking the Small Group Tightrope* by Bill Donahue and Russ Robinson (pp. 47–66)

The Five Love Languages by Gary Chapman

Coaching Conversation 6: Becoming an Inclusive Community

The Big Idea

To help leaders and their groups invite and include others so that everyone can experience community.

Key Verses

Accept one another, then, just as Christ accepted you, in order to bring praise to God.

—Romans 15:7

I was a stranger and you invited me into your home.

—Matthew 25:35 NLT

Model (for the Coach)

As you prepare for this conversation, consider the following:

Think through groups you have led in the past. What were your struggles and successes in adding new people to your group?

How have you taught, modeled, and encouraged openness in the groups in your care?

Guide

How has being in a small group affected your life? What if you had not been invited into this small group (or any other)? How would your life be different?

What are the worst things that could happen by inviting someone new to be a part of your small group?

What are the best things that could happen by inviting someone new to be a part of your small group?

What struggles or opposition do you encounter within the group when you discuss adding a new person?

Think through your last small group meeting. Did anything happen there that might make a new person feel uncomfortable? What changes need to be made so a new member would feel more welcome?

Envision

Spend time with your leaders reflecting on the following quotes from Scripture and Christian authors.

Go out and train everyone you meet, far and near, in this way of life, marking them by baptism in the threefold name: Father, Son, and Holy Spirit. Then instruct them in the practice of all I have commanded you. I'll be with you as you do this, day after day after day, right up to the end of the age.

—Matthew 28:19–20 MSG

But how can people call for help if they don't know who to trust? And how can they know who to trust if they haven't heard of the One who can be trusted? And how can they hear if nobody tells them? And how is anyone going to tell them, unless someone is sent to do it?

—Romans 10:14–15 MSG

A loving community is attractive. And a community which is attractive is by definition welcoming. Life brings new life … Love can never be static. A human heart is either progressing or regressing. If it is not becoming more open, it is closing and withering spiritually. A community which refuses to welcome — whether through fear, weariness, insecurity, a desire to cling to comfort, or just because it is fed up with visitors — is dying spiritually.

—Jean Vanier, *Community and Growth*

The great enemy of community is exclusivity. Groups that exclude others because they are poor or doubters or divorced or sinners or of some other race or nationality are not communities: they are cliques — actually defensive bastions against community ... True communities, if they want to remain such are always reaching to extend themselves. The burden of proof falls on exclusivity. Communities do not ask "How can we justify taking this person in?" Instead the question is "Is it at all justifiable to keep this person out?"   —Scott Peck, "The True Meaning of Community"

Show me a nurturing group not regularly open to new life, and I will guarantee that it's dying. If cells are units of redemption, then no one can button up the lifeboats and hang out a sign, "You can't come in here." The notion of group members shutting themselves off in order to accomplish discipleship is a scourge that will destroy any church's missionary mandate.

—Carl George, *Prepare Your Church for the Future*

- What do these passages show you about the heart of God and inclusivity?
- Where do these thoughts challenge your leadership and your group?

Equip

Resources that can help your leaders grow in this area include:

"Adding Members to Your Group" in *Leading Life-Changing Small Groups* (pp. 161–66)

"Guess Who's Coming to Small Group!" in *Walking the Small Group Tightrope* (pp. 137–58)

Small Group Outreach: Turning Groups Inside Out by Jeffrey Arnold

Coaching Conversation 7: Reaching Out to Seekers

The Big Idea

To help leaders and their groups develop relationships with seekers, to understand each seeker's story, and to determine the best ways to impact that person with God's love so seekers can experience a personal relationship with Christ.

Key Verses

I will search for the lost and bring back the strays. —Ezekiel 34:16

For Christ's love compels us, because we are convinced that one died for all, and therefore all died. And he died for all, that those who live should no longer live for themselves but for him who died for them and was raised again. —2 Corinthians 5:14–15

We are therefore Christ's ambassadors, as though God were making his appeal through us. —2 Corinthians 5:20

Therefore go and make disciples of all nations, baptizing them in the name of the Father and of the Son and of the Holy Spirit, and teaching them to obey everything I have commanded you. And surely I am with you always, to the very end of the age. —Matthew 28:19–20

Model (for the Coach)

As you prepare for this conversation, consider the following:

Think carefully about your own life and your evangelistic temperature. List the names of three people you know who are seekers or are not in a relationship with God. What steps are you taking to build a relationship with them? What are you doing to initiate spiritual conversations with them?

How do your own personal challenges in this area reflect the challenges your leaders may be facing?

Guide

What does it mean to be an ambassador for Christ? How would our lives be different if we lived in such a way?

How can we tell God's story to the world around us? What methods work for you?

What roles do small groups play in sharing this message?

How might your group react to the idea of inviting a seeker to join?

Think through relationships at work, in your neighborhood, or within your family. Who are the people that might be open to Christ or to community?

When is the last time you reminded your group of the need to share Christ's love with the world?

Envision

Consider together these ideas for building the value of evangelism in the group.

Choose a Curriculum That Promotes Evangelism

Do a study on grace.

Study contemporary issues in evangelism.

Study Jesus' reactions to various people groups.

Continually apply the Bible to the world around us.

Lead Your Group in Service Projects

Set the example in showing Christ's love for the world.

Be consistent. Service projects are not reserved just for the holiday seasons.

Pray for Lost People by Name

An empty chair in the room can be a simple reminder to pray for those who don't know God.

Dialogue with the leader about what a seeker needs in a small group (Garry Poole, *Building Contagious Groups*):

To be accepted where they are

To be listened to and understood

To be drawn out patiently

To be cared for and served

To be prayed for

- What next steps can you take as a leader to meet the needs of seekers?
- What next steps can you encourage group members to take?

Equip

Resources that can help your leaders grow in this area include:

"Adding Seekers to Small Groups" in *Leading Life-Changing Small Groups* (p. 166)

Seeker Small Groups by Garry Poole

Small Group Outreach: Turning Groups Inside Out by Jeffrey Arnold

Coaching Conversation 8: Developing Future Leaders

The Big Idea

To help leaders develop a new generation of leaders so that Christ's redemptive purposes can be accomplished in our lives, in our groups, and in our community.

Key Verses

Pass on what you heard from me ... to reliable leaders who are competent to teach others.

—2 Timothy 2:2 MSG

It was [God] who gave some to be apostles, some to be prophets, some to be evangelists, and some to be pastors and teachers, to prepare God's people for works of service so that the body of Christ may be built up until we all reach unity in the faith and in the knowledge of the Son of God and become mature, attaining to the whole measure of the fullness of Christ.   —Ephesians 4:11–13 NIV

As each part does its own special work, it helps the other parts grow, so that the whole body is healthy and growing and full of love.   —Ephesians 4:16 NLT

He appointed twelve—designating them apostles—that they might be with him and that he might send them out to preach.   —Mark 3:14 NIV

Model (for the Coach)

As you prepare for this conversation, consider the following:

If your own path into leadership involved serving as an apprentice, how did you benefit from that experience?

Think of a group leader who has successfully developed and launched an apprentice leader. What principles and practices from this leader's story might be helpful to share with your leader as you meet?

How are you developing your apprentice coach? What successes and struggles are you experiencing?

Guide

What steps have you taken to identify an apprentice leader in your group? What struggles have you had?

What strengths, weaknesses, and motivations do you observe in your apprentice?

What experiences, opportunities, and tasks are you using to develop the leadership and interpersonal skills of your apprentice?

How are you helping your apprentice grow spiritually?

How are you using the time between meetings to develop your apprentice?

Envision

Examine the relationship between Jesus and the apostles in the Gospels. What did Jesus do to develop them in all areas so they were ready to lead?

Spend time with your leaders reflecting on the following quotes from Christian authors.

▶

A man has truly begun to understand the meaning of life when he plants shade trees under which he knows he will never sit.

—Elton Trueblood

If I am to be someone's apprentice, there is one absolutely essential condition. I must be *with* that person. This is true of the student teacher relationship in all generality. And it is precisely what it meant to follow Jesus when he was here in human form. To follow him, in the first place, meant to be with him.

—Dallas Willard, *The Divine Conspiracy*

If you were to live out the concepts described above, how would they impact your relationship with your apprentice leader?

Equip

Resources that can help your leaders grow in this area include:

"Apprentice Development" in *Leading Life-Changing Small Groups* (pp. 67–74)

"Recruit a Leader-in-Training" in *Nine Keys to Effective Small Group Leadership* by Carl George

Leadership Huddles

Imagine what it would be like to stand before an orchestra as its conductor. Seated in front of you are talented musicians, each with their own abilities and unique interests. The instruments they play are as varied as the people who hold them. You hear them warming up and the sounds are disjointed.

As the conductor, your task is to blend all their talents, abilities, and knowledge into a coordinated effort. Following a musical score, you direct them to produce sounds in harmony with each other, resulting in beautiful music.

Leading a huddle can be like conducting an orchestra. Each of your leaders is unique; every leader has different talents and gifts. One may have years of leadership experience while another is a brand new leader. Each leader can play their own rendition of the music and lead a group with their own, unique style. But all of these efforts will seem disjointed unless someone blends them together.

In a huddle, coaches bring together all of this talent, ability, giftedness, and strength. You inspire the leaders to "play together"—to learn from you and from each other how to lead life-changing small groups. And just as the conductor follows a musical score, you follow a plan to develop your leaders. Together you learn from each other, support each other, and develop a team approach to ministry.

A Learning Community

The goal of a huddle is to establish a learning community. Both learning and community are concepts important to the success of your huddles.

Huddles offer the opportunity for leaders to learn new skills. As a coach you should work to create a safe environment in your huddles where leaders feel the freedom to try, practice, and fail—all key components to good training. If leaders are learning, then huddles will have value, and over time their interest in attending huddles will grow.

Huddles also offer the unique opportunity to build community with your leaders. Such settings may be the only times you gather all of your leaders together. Leaders have a passion for community and often connect at a deep level in huddle times. Encourage these connections by planning time in your huddle for the leaders to share experiences and to encourage each other. If you build community, then leaders will have ownership of the huddle and, again, their interest in participating in huddles will increase.

Biblical Examples of Huddles

Several times in Scripture we see groups of leaders gathered together in order to carry out effective ministry. Here are a few examples.

Acts 6: A disagreement arose in the church in Jerusalem. Though we are not given the details, it appears that the twelve apostles met privately to problem-solve before the final solution was announced. They called the church together to share a plan of action they had worked out together. The result was the selection of seven new servant leaders to take on significant ministry roles; new members were added to the leadership team.

Acts 15: Leaders come together in the Council at Jerusalem to problem solve and make strategic decisions. There was a sharp disagreement between leaders, and it was in the context of a leadership meeting that the disagreement was resolved and the unity of the body preserved.

Mark 3: Following a time of ministry, Jesus withdraws from the crowds. As he often did, Jesus took the disciples away to be alone with him so that he could encourage and train them in ministry.

Luke 10: Jesus appoints and sends out seventy-two people into various towns to talk about the kingdom of God. Before they leave, he commissions them, trains them, and prays for them. When they return, he listens to their stories, affirms their efforts, focuses their attention on the proper measurements for success, and offers a prayer of thanksgiving.

Planning a Leadership Huddle

Each huddle that you plan will have a different emphasis. For example, one meeting might focus on community, helping leaders get to know each other better and establish trusting relationships. Another might include an extended time of prayer, and yet another might train leaders in how to find and develop an apprentice leader. You will determine what to emphasize in each huddle based on the needs of your leaders.

Some needs may be obvious at first, but as you prayerfully consider these questions, you will probably identify many areas of need. Remember, the overall purpose of coaching is to shepherd, equip, and reproduce group leaders. Here are some questions to consider as you prepare:

Nurture the Soul
- What exercises or activities can I do to build community with my leaders so they can discuss personal needs or struggles?
- How can I utilize this time to encourage them?
- How should worship and/or prayer be included in the huddle?
- What can we celebrate in both the leaders' group life and personal life?

Develop the Skills
- With what leadership skills do my leaders need help? (New ideas on relationship building, asking creative questions, listening skills, ways to pray as a group, etc.)
- What insights have I gained from visiting groups and from one-on-one conversations that would benefit all my leaders?

- How can I help my leaders learn from each other's experiences?
- What problems are my leaders encountering and how can we work together in the huddle to explore solutions?

Build the Team

- Can my leaders impart the vision for the small group ministry to their group members? How would they explain this vision?
- In what areas do my leaders need to be challenged?
- What ministry goals and expectations need an update or accountability check-in (developing an apprentice, adding new group members, etc.)?
- What information do my leaders need about future meetings, church-wide events, training opportunities, and updates?

Planning a huddle is like piecing together a puzzle. You will not be able to deal with every issue and every need in each huddle. So ask yourself, "What do my leaders need *most* from this time together?" Then plan accordingly. Remember to always *ask* your leaders what their needs are. It is an obvious but often overlooked question.

A Quick Test for Value

After you plan your huddle meeting, use this quick checklist to measure the value your meeting will have to your leaders. See the meeting through your leader's eyes and ask these questions about your upcoming huddle:

- Is it worth my time and effort?
- Am I going to feel encouraged?
- Will it meet my needs?
- Will I learn something new?
- Will I have the opportunity to participate?

If your leaders will answer yes to these questions, then you have planned a good huddle!

Conducting Huddles

Here are some guidelines for how you will nurture, develop, and build your leaders in the huddle time.

Nurturing Leaders in the Huddle

Leaders should feel the freedom to share personal and leadership issues in the safety of the huddle. Set the tone that both successes and struggles are welcome. However, recognize that some issues are better dealt with in the one-on-one setting than in the huddle.

Here are some guidelines to help determine the best place to deal with issues that may arise in the huddle. In all cases, be sensitive to the leading of the Holy Spirit when deciding how to handle each issue.

In the Huddle

- Never ignore or dismiss a need that someone brings to the huddle.
- Be an example of a caring leader to your huddle members.
- Encourage group members to support one another and help each other problem-solve.
- Allow huddle members to ask questions and challenge each other.
- Encourage huddle members to pray for each other during the huddle and between meetings.

At Another Time

- If the leader raises a personal issue, offer to discuss it at another time unless the person desires to discuss it with the huddle.
- If there is a complex issue, one that would take a long time to resolve, schedule a different time to fully discuss it.
- If there is a unique situation to which no one else can relate, discuss it at another time.
- If confidences would be violated in any way, do not discuss the matter. Even the best leaders will at times have to fight the urge to share inappropriately. When leaders break the confidential nature of their group (gossip), they teach the huddle members that they can't be trusted. Such confidence breaking will discourage deeper sharing in your huddles.
- If you are not sure, wait until you know more about the issue to discuss it in the huddle.

Three Aspects of Nurturing Leaders

Observe what your leaders are saying about their growth and struggles in each of these areas. Be an encourager whenever possible.

1. Spiritual

- How are their quiet times?
- What do they feel God is teaching them lately?
- Are they struggling with any sin or other issue?
- Is their relationship with Jesus growing?
- Do they view each activity of life as a means of learning from Christ?

2. Relational

- Are their family relationships strong?
- How is their relationship with the other leaders in the huddle?
- How do they relate to the people in their small group?
- How is their relationship with you?

3. Personal

- What personal issues are occupying their time and energy?
- What are their recent struggles and successes?

Leadership Huddle Planning Guide

Huddle Date: July 20   **Time:** 7-9 PM   **Place:** Anderson's House

Pray

Spend time in prayer, asking God for insight and guidance as you plan. *I pray that the leaders will continue to have willingness to add new people to their groups.*

Pray for each of your leaders.

Questions to Consider

What are my leaders telling me? *They need ideas for getting members to pray out loud*

What do I need to ask them? *How is the Anderson group adjusting to the new couple?*

What are my objectives for this meeting? *To build relationships, pray, and encourage spiritual growth.*

Where is the Holy Spirit leading me? *To develop the relationships between the leaders.*

Categories		Need/Issue	Time
Nurture	Community	Do a relationship-building exercise to encourage authenticity.	45 min.
	Encouragement		
	Worship/Prayer	Prayer and worship to begin the huddle.	15 min.
	Celebration	Andersons added a new couple, Smith's new apprentice.	10 min.
Develop	Skill Training	Introduce creative ideas for group prayer.	30 min.
	Insights		
	Idea Exchange	Invite leaders to share best/worst prayer ideas.	10 min.
	Problem Solving		
Build	Vision		
	Challenge		
	Accountability		
	Communication	New curriculum ideas, next 3 huddle dates	

Leadership Huddle Planning Guide

Huddle Date: **Time:**   **Place:**

Pray
Spend time in prayer, asking God for insight and guidance as you plan.

Pray for each of your leaders.

Questions to Consider
What are my leaders telling me?

What do I need to ask them?

What are my objectives for this meeting?

Where is the Holy Spirit leading me?

Categories		Need/Issue	Time
Nurture	Community		
	Encouragement		
	Worship/Prayer		
	Celebration		
Develop	Skill Training		
	Insights		
	Idea Exchange		
	Problem Solving		
Build	Vision		
	Challenge		
	Accountability		
	Communication		

Developing Skills in the Huddle

Here are three steps you can take to maximize the huddle time for skill development:

1. Identify the Skill

One-on-one conversations and visiting the leaders' groups will help you assess which skill set needs to be developed or improved in your leaders. Some ideas for skill development might be:

- Effectively using icebreaker questions
- Relationship-building exercises
- Using the Bible effectively in groups
- Listening skills
- Writing and asking good questions
- Leading group prayer
- Dealing with talkative or shy members
- Choosing and using curriculum
- Managing group dynamics

2. Model the Skill

- Try out new leadership practices or techniques in the huddle.
- Adults learn best by doing. Don't just teach the skill; give leaders a chance to try it for themselves.
- After leaders have experimented with these skills in the huddle, encourage them to take the same ideas and methods back to their group.

3. Involve Others

- If there is a leader who is very strong in a given skill, invite them to help train the other leaders. For example, if someone has done some creative things with prayer in their small group, ask them to use their ideas to lead the prayer time in the huddle.
- As a coach you will not have experienced everything that your leaders will face in their groups. Nor will you be strong in every skill your leaders need. If you encourage the leaders to share experiences and ideas, the leaders will learn to value each other and ask the other leaders for help with problems.

Building the Leadership Team in the Huddle

Vision

Leaders will look to their coach to recast and clarify the vision for community and small groups. They will look to your lead in carrying out the vision. But there are different levels of response in understanding and owning that vision.

1. Leaders must first understand the vision. Do they comprehend the facts? Is the vision clear?
2. Leaders must be fully convinced, beyond mere facts, that the vision is important. Do they believe in the vision?
3. Leaders must be participating, knowing that God is calling them to do this. Are they giving their best effort to build life-changing small groups?
4. Leaders must be passing on their understanding of and their passion for the vision. Are they passing the vision on to the group? To their apprentice?

Knowing where each leader is on the continuum will help you discern your next steps and how to best utilize your huddles to re-cast or clarify the vision so you can take them to the next level.

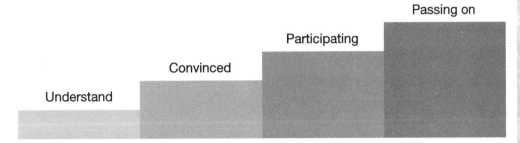

Apprentice Development

In order for more people to be able to grow in their relationship with Christ through small groups, apprentice coaches and leaders must be developed for future groups and huddles.

Apprentice Coaches

Model for your leaders the vision and the value of apprentice development. Involve your apprentice coach in every aspect of the ministry:

- Assessing needs
- Planning the huddles
- Leading the huddles
- Evaluating the huddles
- Conducting one-on-one meetings
- Visiting groups

During huddles, allow your apprentice to lead in areas that you have agreed upon. After the huddle, provide encouragement and suggestions.

Apprentice Leaders

In general, it is good to include apprentice group leaders in leadership huddles. Here are some considerations to help determine when apprentice attendance would not be appropriate:

- The huddle size grows too large to be effective.
- You have no apprentice coach to share huddle leadership responsibilities.
- The topic of conversation is not appropriate for apprentice leaders.

When apprentice leaders attend huddles, remember that the leader (not you) takes primary responsibility for training the apprentice. You provide help, but the leader should be the primary developer.

Provide your leaders with the resources they need to develop their apprentice. This may include books, video or audio tapes, people resources, or assistance with a problem.

Evaluating Huddles

As soon as possible after your huddle, take a few minutes to answer the questions below. They will help you evaluate the effectiveness of your meeting and will assist you as you plan your next huddle. If you have an apprentice coach, evaluate your huddle together. You may also want to invite the leaders to share their evaluation.

- What went well? What did not go well?
- Was there enough time for each exercise or activity?
- How could the huddle experience be improved?
- How did the huddle help build community with the leaders?
- Did the leaders feel encouraged?
- Did the huddle have value for the leaders?
- What items from the huddle need follow-up?

▶ Development Aid ▶

Coaching Huddles

Coaching huddles are leadership gatherings designed around eight key practices for small group leaders that we believe are essential to their growth and effectiveness. Here are the eight practices again to refresh your memory:

- Modeling Personal Growth
- Shepherding Your Leaders
- Building Authentic Relationships
- Resolving Conflict in a Healthy Manner
- Extending Care and Compassion
- Becoming an Inclusive Community
- Reaching Out to Seekers
- Developing Future Leaders

For your reference, we have included some common components for each huddle that you lead. Obviously, all huddles will not look the same and should never have a regimented or mechanical feel. But we wanted to give you a framework to organize and develop the huddle. You should vary the order from time to time. Huddles should not be predictable or routine. Some of the creativity you use will simply be varying the order and time spent for each huddle segment.

Each huddle is designed to help coaches utilize the four key practices of coaching: Modeling, Guiding, Envisioning, and Equipping.

Model: A time for building community and checking in personally. This can help set the tone and help leaders develop relationships. Remember that leaders see your life and may follow your example—or lack thereof.

Guide: Help leaders grow spiritually by sharing Scripture, telling stories, and asking questions that prompt them to take a next step in personal and ministry growth.

Envision: This may include prayer, storytelling, and worship so that God is recognized as the source for all ministry growth. It involves pointing to the future and reminding each other that God will continue to do his work through us by his grace.

Equip: Work together to solve problems, develop creative ideas, share experiences, and brainstorm for the future direction of the ministry. This may also involve the imparting of a skill or connecting leaders to resources that will help them become more effective.

Huddle 1: Modeling Personal Growth

Focus: To help your small group leaders model a Christian life that is characterized by the ways and teachings of Jesus Christ.

Key Passage: 1 Timothy 4:11–16

Goal: To guide leaders through a spiritual inventory that allows them to "pay close attention to themselves" as Paul exhorts Timothy to do.

Materials Needed: Paper and Bibles

Logistics: Consider serving refreshments, and if possible, choose a place that allows for some quiet reflection.

Guide

Begin the huddle with prayer and guide your leaders into a time of thankfulness and expectation for your time together. Ask God to help your minds slow down and focus on the time you have as a leadership community.

1. Take about ten minutes to discuss the weeks since your last contact. Ask leaders for brief, personal updates—how they are doing on a scale of one to five, with five meaning strong and energized, and one meaning depleted or tired.

2. Ask an opening question: What does it mean to be an example to others of the spiritual life one should lead? Is it overwhelming? Intimidating? In light of how each leader is doing, is this an impossible task? Do leaders understand that the power of Christ is revealed through us, that we are but clay jars? Remind them that they are examples in success and in failure. We do not hide our failures but we let Christ redeem them for growth in our lives.

3. Read 1 Timothy 4:11–16 and discuss the implications of the passage. Note that Paul emphasizes both the opportunity and obligation Timothy has as a leader.

Model

4. Look at the items in verse 12 and use them as a kind of spiritual inventory. Ask members to examine their lives in each area: speech, life, love, faith, and purity. If they could develop in one area over the next thirty days, what might that be? How are these areas integrated?

Speech: How I use words

Life: How I face trials and decisions

Love: How I engage in relationships

Faith: How I trust Christ for strength and connect with him

Purity: How I face my sin and grow in character

5. Spend time encouraging one another to pursue a life like Christ's with an attitude of surrender. Remind leaders that they are not perfect, and that we all need to come before God each day and renew our commitment to him, confessing sin and asking for strength and power for the day ahead. Remember the Holy Spirit is at work. Show leaders what you are doing to follow Christ, how you come to him for strength, and that you also need his healing grace.

Envision

6. Take a few minutes to tell your leaders how their intentional pursuit of character growth and purity will have a ripple effect on their small group members. Look again at 1 Timothy 4:16 where it is clear that Timothy's work will not only have a personal benefit (save him from a life of sin and disobedience)

but will also benefit the lives of others (it will save them from living in ways that destroy them spiritually and hurt the church in Ephesus).

Joe Stowell spoke the following quote, "It takes a changing life to change a life" in a message he gave to a group of small group leaders years ago. You might read this to your leaders and encourage them to be the kind of person who has a changing life.

Equip

7. Recommend the spiritual discipline of self and peer examination periodically. For self-examination, leaders can simply have a quiet time for reflection on a regular basis, asking the Spirit to point out areas of weakness as well as areas of strength. For peer examination, encourage leaders to have a "spiritual friendship" with someone they trust who can speak into their life. Someone who can give them feedback about their character, attitude, behavior patterns, spiritual gifts, and development as a leader. Ideally, a mentor would be a great person to do this.

Also recommend some additional reading like *Spiritual Leadership* by J. Oswald Sanders which focuses on the character and practices of a Christ-honoring leader.

A great Bible passage to read and reflect on is John 15:1–17.

Huddle 2: Shepherding Your Leaders

Focus: To help leaders feel comfortable with their role as a spiritual guide in the life of others.

Key Passage: Matthew 22:34–40

Goal: To provide leaders with a simple way to guide others into a deeper relationship with Christ.

Materials Needed: Paper and Bibles

Logistics: Consider having the huddle in a place where leaders can sit around tables or in a circle for better group discussion.

Model

Connect for a few minutes with some refreshments and catch up on one another's week. Make this time light and informal to set a relaxed and less structured tone.

1. Pray for leaders in your group by name. Call out to God on behalf of or with each one based on the needs and strengths they have. In this way you will model how to pray specifically for people at a group meeting. It is powerful to pray for someone in the presence of others, and it models your knowledge of their lives, your interest in their needs, and your passion for their growth and success.

Guide

2. First, gather your leaders into a circle and ask them to read Matthew 28:19–20. Since we are to obey all that Jesus commanded, have them list as many commandments as possible that Jesus gave his followers. (There are actually several hundred, but we want to show them that Jesus boiled all his commands down to two.)

3. Now ask leaders to read Matthew 22:34–40. What is the focus of all of Jesus' commands?

4. Group Discussion: Ask leaders to share together for a few moments around these questions: How do you feel about being a "spiritual guide" of sorts, moving people forward in their relationship with Christ? Do you feel inadequate? Excited? Nervous? Grateful?

Envision

5. Help leaders see that guiding people is simple, in that it all comes down to loving God and loving others. Encourage leaders to remember this. It's all about relationships, both with God and with other people. That is why their small group ministry is so essential. It has a strong focus on relationships and helps their members grow in relational health to God and to other members, as well as to those outside the group (unsaved friends, family, fellow believers in the church, and so on).

Equip

6. Leaders might want to have this same "love God, love others" discussion with their groups. The following is a way to help them do that.

Question for a small group: What does it look like to love God? To love others? Give the small group a simple exercise for this discussion. Go to Exodus 20:1–17 (The Ten Commandments) and ask members to divide the commandments into the two categories below. Then, as a small group, discuss how the group *together* can help one another become more loving. Describe practical ways to express:

1. Love to God
2. Love to others

Huddle 3: Building Authentic Relationships

Focus: To give leaders the confidence to guide discussions.

Key Passages: Proverbs 17:27–28; 18:13

Goal: To equip leaders to create an environment that promotes discussion in their groups.

Materials Needed: DVD or video player, Bibles

Logistics: Some snacks and a room to watch the DVD/video

(*Note to Coaches:* Choose a four- to six-minute movie or TV clip that shows a group discussion or argument. It could be a popular TV show or movie. The discussion could be a great one or a poor one, where people interrupt and do not listen well. It does not matter. But the more interaction, the better. Use discretion regarding language, content of the film, movie rating, and so on. No need to create unnecessary conflict or distract from the point of the meeting.)

Spend a few minutes to connect relationally and greet each other. Keep this brief unless there is a crisis to deal with.

Envision

1. Begin this session with some vision casting. Ask, "What would it look like to have a group discussion flow so well that you, the leader, could leave the room for twenty minutes and when you return, the discussion is still going on and no one knows you ever left?" What would the elements of such a discussion look like?

Take a few minutes to list these responses on paper.

Guide

2. Show the TV/movie clip and ask members if they see anything they listed (qualities of a good discussion) in the clip. What are the communication patterns like? How would they lead this discussion if it were a meeting? What role does listening play?

3. Read Proverbs 17:27–28 and 18:13. What key to facilitation is taught in these verses?

4. What does it feel like to be listened to and to be *really* heard? How do we know that we have been heard and understood?

Model

5. As you lead this discussion as a coach, make sure you model good listening skills. Ask good questions. Show genuine interest. Use phrases like, "Tell us more about that" and "Why do you feel so strongly about that?" Listen to body language and people's tone of voice. Watch their energy level as they talk. Observe who talks the most. Consider how to draw others into the conversation. "Sarah, would you add anything to what has been said so far?"

If you want to have some fun, model poor listening skills. Interrupt people, just nod a lot and say, "Uh huh" but ask no follow-up questions. Change the subject quickly and then spend more time talking about your own feelings and experiences. After a time, stop the huddle meeting and ask leaders what they observed about what you just did. Ask if they do this in groups, becoming so focused on the agenda that they cannot really listen to the feelings, interests, and words of members.

Equip

Recommend the Listening Skills section in the book *Leading Life-Changing Small Groups* as a guide. It compares active versus passive listening and the results of each.

Take a few minutes to simply practice listening and asking good follow-up questions. Ask someone to be the observer and give feedback to leaders after this exercise. Have some fun with this.

Remind leaders to pay attention to what is happening in the circle when there is a discussion going on. Who is talking? Who is getting ignored? Who feels scared? Who needs encouragement? What kind of questions are being asked? Remember that closed questions, questions that have right and wrong answers or are questions of "fact," will not generate much discussion. Open questions—questions of feeling, opinions, reactions, ideas—invite people to talk and express their thoughts and open their hearts.

Huddle 4: Resolving Conflict in a Healthy Manner

Focus: Addressing conflict and helping people speak the truth in love.

Key Passages: Matthew 18:15–18; Ephesians 4:25–32

Goal: To equip leaders to engage in conflict as it arises and to face conflict with grace and truth.

Materials Needed: Bibles and some 3 x 5 cards or paper

Logistics: Contact one of your leaders ahead of time and ask them to bring a "case study" of a conflict situation either in personal life or in group life. No names. Make sure confidentiality is honored. Debrief this with them before asking them to bring it to the group. Ask them to limit their example to one page, to type it, if possible, and to have copies for the group. If this is not appropriate, create a case study yourself.

The case should include a brief statement of the situation, the background of the conflict, and the process that took place. Include the reactions and responses of those involved. DO NOT describe the resolution yet. Just describe the tension and the problem. In your meeting you will explore solutions and then see what really happened.

Model

1. Begin with sharing a story of a relational breakdown in your life (not your case study if you are bringing one to the huddle). This could be a conflict at work, a friendship while growing up, or a family situation. Describe how you dealt with it, where you failed in addressing the conflict appropriately, and what you did well. Stories are great ways to encourage others, to show your own failures and humility, and to model the practice of storytelling for other leaders who are watching you.

As you do this you also model what is appropriate self-disclosure and confidentiality (how you describe the conflict without embarrassing or violating the confidence of those who were involved in it).

2. Pray for courage for each leader to face the difficult aspects of group life as conflicts arise or as difficult people enter a group and create tension.

Equip

3. Hand each leader a 3 x 5 card and ask them to write down what they believe is the key to facing relational tension in groups. What is important to do and not to do? Collect the cards and see as a group if you can prioritize what they have shared.

4. Check the list against Ephesians 4:25–32 and the process of Matthew 18:15–18.

5. Now distribute the case study and have leaders in groups of two to three discuss the situation and see what they would do. After talking about the case, read the actual results of what happened. Was the conflict resolved? Is it still being worked on? What is at stake? How do the participants feel now? Is there complete reconciliation? If not, why? If so, what made this happen?

Envision

6. Help leaders see that conflict can be met with grace and truth. We speak in love to one another but do not hold back truth. We courageously face the relational breakdowns that threaten our oneness in Christ (John 17:20–23) and the health of our groups. Envision your leaders to have hope—many conflicts work out over time with the right biblical process and attitude. But some do not, and we need to be prepared to work through that result as well, whether that involves the whole process of Matthew 18:15–18 or not.

Encourage members not to fear conflict; rather, fear avoiding it when it should be dealt with. Running away from conflict will destroy a group or a relationship.

▶

Guide

7. Lead your huddle members in a time of prayer. Ask them to write the names of people in their group or in their lives that they must meet with to begin the process of healthy conflict resolution. Remind them that they, too, model how to handle conflict to their own members. If they do not honor the biblical process, the group will see and probably ignore the process as well.

Ask them to speak with their groups, asking members (individually or as a small group) to evaluate how well the group is doing facing tension when it arises. What steps could the group take to improve the way they handle relational challenges? Who needs to extend forgiveness?

Huddle 5: Extending Care and Compassion

Focus: To discover creative ways to grow the servant hearts of leaders.

Key Passage: Matthew 9:35–38

Goal: To identify serving opportunities and evaluate our hearts for compassion.

Materials Needed: News magazines

Logistics: Consider having your huddle at a place where there is great need in your community.

Guide

1. Begin with a time of prayer for people who are in need of help and compassion. Ask members to name friends or situations that require prayer for social, physical, and financial help.

2. Read Matthew 9:35–38 and ask, "What is the focus of the shepherds Jesus is looking for?"

Envision

3. Ask members to take magazines and cut out some photos that show people in need—the poor, hungry, refugees, children without parents, war victims, and so on. What images come to mind?

4. What do you feel when you see these photos? What happens to your heart? How does your heart connect with Jesus' heart as he looked over Jerusalem?

5. What would it look like if our churches and our small groups could reach out and meet some of these needs? What kinds of needs can be addressed right in our own neighborhoods or near our church? What might that look like?

Equip

6. Take some extended time to help leaders evaluate the gifts and passions of group members and the needs in their communities.

   1. My group members
   2. Community needs
   3. Our opportunities

Ask leaders to spend a few minutes on this alone, then gather your huddle together to see what each leader sees as opportunities their group could act on. What are the common needs? How could groups come together to meet these needs? How could your entire huddle of leaders act collectively to meet the needs in a community, mobilizing all the groups represented by this huddle toward the same end?

Read Matthew 26:31–46 to understand how important this is to Christ.

Model

7. This is an opportunity for us as leaders to lead the way, to show our heart of compassion for the poor, lost, lonely, and needy folks in our church and neighborhoods. Describe how you are praying for these people, reaching out with your family, giving of your time and resources to help others. Not in a prideful way, but as an example to the other leaders in your huddle that you believe in the cause and are acting on it.

▶

Huddle 6: Becoming an Inclusive Community

Focus: To help develop the practice of inclusion, encouraging leaders to open their groups to people different from themselves.

Key Passage: Psalm 67

Goal: To identify ways of becoming more inclusive as a group.

Materials Needed: DVD/video

Logistics: A place to watch a movie

Envision

1. After some brief checking in and snacks, consider watching a movie that reinforces the need for inclusion or that emphasizes racial reconciliation, the overcoming of oppression, or class struggles. Recommended movies would be *Ghandi, Remember the Titans,* and *Michael Collins* (about Ireland), or you might have another one in mind. If you cannot take the time to show an entire movie, show a lengthy clip that is powerful. Twenty to thirty minutes is good.

2. Debrief the film. What motivated the people to fight against injustice and seek to be included? How might it feel to be "on the outside" looking in?

Guide

3. Take time to pray for a heart for those of other races, creeds, colors, and experiences. Ask God to open wide the hearts of your small group leaders so they can begin to model this inclusion for their groups.

4. Read Psalm 67. Even though Israel was God's chosen people, what is the heart of God for the nations? How can we develop such a heart? What other materials (like *Divided by Faith* by Michael O. Emerson and Christian Smith) can we read to understand the plight of those who are not part of the power structure of our country?

Equip

5. Spend time brainstorming what "inclusivity" would look like in the small groups represented in the huddle. What does it take to open our groups? How do we build personal relationships that model this openness?

6. Invite someone from a different faith, race, background, or viewpoint to come to your huddle. Interview them. What is important to them? How can a church help them? What would they want us to know about them? About others like them?

7. What is the church already doing that your small groups can connect to so that people's hearts for inclusivity grow?

Model

8. Begin to pray for and develop relationships yourself. List some people you could get to know better at work or in the community. It may be a business person or a single parent or a missionary on furlough who has experiences in other cultures.

Huddle 7: Reaching Out to Seekers

Focus: To help leaders gain a heart for the lost and help their groups develop the same.

Key Passages: Ezekiel 34:16; Luke 15

Goal: To pray for and connect with opportunities to reach people who are far from God.

Materials Needed: Paper and Bibles

Logistics: Consider inviting a non-Christian friend to come to your huddle meeting during the snack or meal time. During this time, ask them to describe their understanding of God and their view of Christians. After the friend(s) leaves, have your meeting and discuss their comments.

Model

1. Describe the relationships you are developing with non-Christians and what priority they have in your life. If this is an area of weakness for you, simply admit that and make a commitment to improve. Ask the other leaders for accountability and for prayer as you move ahead. List the names of people you love and care for who do not know God, and ask leaders to do the same. Using only first names, pray for these people.

Guide

2. Read Luke 15 and ask your group leaders what they notice about the three parables. What is Jesus trying to show us about the heart of the Father toward those who are strays, wandering from him?

3. What is their attitude toward those far from God?

4. If you invited a seeker for dinner, what did they say? How do you feel toward them?

Envision

5. Remind leaders that within two years of becoming a Christian, most believers lose all significant contact with the unchurched and have no close unchurched friends. How can we remedy this?

6. What would it look like to our groups if each small group represented in the huddle would befriend two people over the next year, build a relationship with them, invite them to social outings, and to church? What impact might that have? What if each member of each small group did that? You could impact forty to fifty people!

Equip

7. Encourage members to take an evangelism training course like *Becoming a Contagious Christian* so they know how to build relationships and share their faith with lost people in an intentional but not oppressive way. Take a few moments to share ways to start spiritual conversations with people. Consider inviting someone who works regularly with lost people to come to the huddle or to leaders' groups to share their stories and vision. Consider reading a brief book together as a small group to help people catch a vision for seekers and to build a relationship with people they already know who are not connected to Christ.

Huddle 8: Developing Future Leaders

Focus: The ministry continues when we invest in others toward leadership.

Key Passages: Mark 3:14; 2 Timothy 2:2

Goal: To identify potential leaders and the process to build into them.

Materials Needed: Paper and Bibles

Logistics: A simple meeting room or a home, refreshments

Model

1. As a coach, describe for your huddle a time when someone built into you. What was the effect? Are they a mentor today? Then ask the leaders to describe a situation of their own.

2. Describe what you look for in an apprentice, someone you would invest time in.

Envision

3. What would happen in our church if every existing small group leader identified and built into just one other person in the coming year? If that one person is a leader, how many new groups would that generate? How many people would now have an opportunity to experience group life?

If you have an apprentice, bring the apprentice to the huddle. Let leaders in the huddle meet the person (people) you are developing.

Help leaders see that they can invite others to "grow" into leadership instead of jumping into it right away. Becoming a leader is a process, and there is time to grow under the supervision and encouragement of others who are leading now.

Equip

4. Find a leader in your church who is good at developing others, either in the church or in the workplace. Interview them. What do they look for? How do they start? What should we be careful of when inviting others into leadership?

5. Spend time creating a list of potential leaders in your church. Now list the obstacles that are keeping them from leading. Is it training, vision, skills, fear, past experience? Now brainstorm ways to address those obstacles.

6. Consider bringing a formerly "reluctant" leader to the huddle or to a training session for leaders at the church. Ask the leader what helped them take the plunge into leadership. Who helped them?

Guide

7. Read 2 Timothy 2:2 and Mark 3:14. What do you notice about what Jesus did and what Paul did? You might also look at Matthew 10 and Luke 10 where Jesus gave people "on-the-job" training as leaders.

8. Pray for spiritual eyes to see potential leaders (they often do not look like "leaders") and for the courage to boldly ask those people to enter a development process, a partnership. Ask them to join a leadership community by attending your huddle so they can see what leaders do. Invite them to a group.

Help the leaders in your huddle see this as a spiritual battle. Matthew 9:35–38 says we need to pray for workers in the harvest. God must move in their hearts, and the Evil One hates leaders—because they start little communities called small groups that can change the world. So pray!

Visiting Groups

Each day, physicians in hospitals around the globe make rounds, checking on patients under their care. They visit these patients to assess their condition, provide information and encouragement, and make suggestions for improvement. They show care to everyone visited, paying attention to each patient's general well-being.

Likewise, coaches are called upon to "make the rounds," visiting each group, paying attention to the well-being of the leader and the group members. Coaches provide care and attempt to correct any health problems in the group. They give information as to what practical steps can be taken to grow as a healthy group.

If done correctly, group members and leaders should feel encouraged after the coach's visit. They will be glad the coach came and will look forward to the next visit. That's the mark of a good shepherd—and a great coach.

The Purpose of Group Visits

In Acts 15:36, Paul and Barnabas decided to go to every city where they had preached the Word of the Lord. Their desire was to encourage the churches, to see how they were doing, and to offer any assistance that was needed. Like Paul and Barnabas, coaches visit groups to see what is being done, to confront any problems, to encourage the group leader and members, and to help groups grow.

You can easily discover the basic facts about a group, such as the curriculum being used, who the group members are, who is leading, and when and where the group meets. Visiting a typical group meeting will give the coach insight into some of the intangibles, such as:

- Are healthy, authentic relationships developing in the group?
- Is there any unhealthy conflict in the group?
- Are group members growing spiritually?
- Is the group welcoming new people and including them in all of group life?
- How is the leader utilizing and developing the apprentice leader?

Keys to Effective Group Visits

An effective group visit will provide support and encouragement to the leader as well as to the group members. To maximize your visit, consider the following needs:

Calm the Leader's Fears

Leaders may have some anxiety about your visit. This is almost always true for the first visit, but hopefully subsides after that. For this reason, it is good to establish a relationship with the leader before visiting the group. Leaders need to know they are important to you, not just because of the ministry they are doing, but because of who they are.

Leaders also need to know that you are there to help them. Assure them that your purpose in visiting the group is to support and encourage them, to be a resource, and to provide ideas for their group. You are *not* there to criticize or point out things they are doing wrong.

While there is accountability involved, the leader should not fear your visit, because your main objectives are to be a mentor and to develop leadership skills.

Be an Encourager

The apostle Paul spent a great deal of his ministry encouraging other leaders and Christ-followers. He so highly valued encouragement that when he could not go personally, he sent Timothy, Silas, or another representative with the primary purpose of encouraging people.

Your leaders need encouragement. Even the most seasoned, successful leaders experience times of discouragement; some may even feel like quitting. Leaders often have no idea the difference their leadership is making in people's lives.

Your group visit will be an encouragement if you:
- Use the 10:2 Rule—provide ten encouraging comments for every two suggestions for improvement.
- Tell group members how much *you* appreciate their leader.
- Give any compliments that are sincere and that you feel comfortable sharing. (For example, "I really appreciate the way everyone shares in the discussion.")
- After the meeting, give the leader specific feedback. What did you appreciate about the way they led the group meeting?

Be Informed

Group visits are most effective when coaches come fully informed regarding the small group and its members. Here are some key things to consider, items you may want to ask the leader in a one-on-one conversation as you plan your first group visit:
- What is the nature and purpose of the group?
- How long has the group been together? How did it start?
- What curriculum is the group using and which lesson are they on?
- What are the names of the group members?
- When would the leader like you to arrive?
- Does the leader have any concerns about this meeting?
- What role should you play in the meeting? Observer? Participant?

Go with a Plan

As you plan your visit to the group, think through your role and how you can best serve this particular leader and group. Commit the time to prayer, asking God to use you to help the leader and the group members grow in their relationship with Christ.

Because you are a guest in the group, the members of the group may change their relating patterns—sharing more or less because of their nervousness.

Coaches should plan regular visits to groups so that members become comfortable with their presence. A good rule of thumb is two to three visits per calendar or ministry year.

Meet with the Leader

Several weeks prior to your group visit, meet with the group leader and the apprentice. This may be part of a regular one-on-one meeting or a separate meeting for the sole purpose of planning your group visit. When you meet, allow time to:

- Explain the purpose of the visit to the leader.
- Select the best day and time for you to visit. Certain types of groups or group studies may require more planning to select an appropriate night for a group visit.
- Answer any questions the leader may have about your visit.
- Get the leader's perception of the current status of the group. Include any concerns, reasons to celebrate, or problems.
- Pray with the leader about his group and your visit.
- Remind the group leader to inform the group members that you will be visiting.

Set Goals

Goals will help you clarify your role during the visit and what action to take with the leader and apprentice. Ask yourself these questions regarding your group visit:

- Why am I visiting this group?
- What do I hope to achieve by this visit?

Here are some possible answers to those questions:

For Myself

> I hope to get to know the leader and group members better.
>
> I hope to gain an understanding of how the leader relates to the group.
>
> I want to see how the leader is developing the apprentice.
>
> I will look for potential leaders and apprentices.
>
> I wish to understand the nature of the relationships in the group.
>
> I will evaluate the commitment level of the members to this group.
>
> I want to develop the skills of my apprentice coach.

For the Leader

> I want to encourage and support this leader.
>
> The leader needs help in assessing a particular situation.
>
> There is an issue or problem the leader needs help solving.
>
> I want to challenge this leader with some new ideas or methods.
>
> I want to affirm this leader's high commitment (or other positive qualities) to group members.
>
> I want to assist the group in birthing (multiplying).
>
> I would like to clarify the vision of small groups.
>
> I want to challenge this group to be open to new members.

For the Group Members

I will help the group understand that they have a coach and staff supporting them.

I will answer questions they might have about the ministry or the church.

I will answer questions about the small group ministry.

I will encourage them in their commitment to attending a small group.

I will affirm their desire to grow in their relationship with Christ.

Plan the Specifics

Use the first page of the planning guide on page 107 to think through the details and the goals for your visit. Fill in the top part of the guide with pertinent facts about your visit. This will also serve as a quick reference during the visit.

Leader's Evaluation: Based on your conversations with the leader, record any observations or insights.

- What is the status of the group?
- What reasons are there to celebrate?
- What concerns or problems did the leader share?
- How is the leader developing the apprentice?

Follow-up Issues: What issues have previously surfaced that you would like to follow up on with this leader and/or group?

The Role of the Coach: What participation level is the leader expecting from you during the group meeting?

Goals: What would you like to accomplish during the visit? Using the previous list, write specific goals in the box.

Making the Group Visit
Arrive Early

Plan to meet with the leader and apprentice before the meeting.

- Ask them how they are doing personally.
- Ask them again about the group. Are there any concerns for the meeting?
- Confirm the role that they would like you to play in the group meeting.
- Discuss the agenda and the leader's plan for the group meeting.
- Pray together for them, for the people in the group, and for the meeting.
- Assure them you are there to support them.
- Greet the group members as they arrive.

Observe the Meeting

Ask the leader to introduce you to the group members and remind the group of why you are there. Participate at the level that you have agreed upon with the leader. Make sure that your participation does not limit or inhibit the participation of the group members. Remember, the goal of the visit is to observe the group in action. Pay close attention to how the leader and the apprentice interact with the group.

The worksheet on page 109 will help you think through how to observe the meeting. Here are some questions you may wish to include when making your observations:

- Was the setting conducive to a good meeting?
- Did the meeting start and end on time?
- Did the leader stay on the subject?
- Was the leader in control but not overbearing?
- Were the questions effective?
- Did the leader listen to the responses?
- How well did the group members relate to each other?
- What is the relationship between the leader and group members?
- Did any group member seem to dominate the discussion?
- Is multiplication (birthing) a part of the group's strategy?
- Is the group open to new people? When was the newest group member added?
- Was the prayer time meaningful? Who participated?
- How was God at work in this meeting?

Be careful about taking notes during the meeting. It may appear that you are being critical of the group in general or of a specific comment made by a group member. It is best to block out some time soon after the meeting to record your observations in private.

Also be prepared to leave during part of the meeting if the group needs to share some confidential thoughts or prayer requests. Step out of the room, or simply leave early, thanking the group for the opportunity to connect with them.

After the Group Visit

After the meeting, give some immediate feedback to the leader and apprentice. Share a couple of specific, encouraging thoughts. Ask questions to clarify any part of the group meeting that was unclear or confusing to you.

Schedule another time to meet with the leader and apprentice as soon as possible after the visit. Review in detail your thoughts and comments, remembering to be encouraging about the things they did well.

Do not simply point out areas of their leadership that need work; be prepared to offer concrete suggestions for improvement. Give several ideas to choose from, so they can decide which would work best in their group. Be a resource for your leaders.

If problems surfaced during your visit, be certain to follow up with the leader as often as needed, even if it is several times each week. Work with the leader to bring resolution to the problem.

After the visit, evaluate your own effectiveness as a coach. Look over your comments and see if there is anything you could have done differently. If your apprentice coach was with you, discuss the visit together.

Keep a record of your visit to review before the next time you sit in on this group. Use this guide as a tool for planning a visit.

My Goals for This Visit

Develop the Skills

The
central way I see
God using me during
this visit is . . .

Nurture the Soul   **Build the Team**

Planning a Group Visit

Group Leader Name	Date	Time of meeting
Group Members	Location	Time to arrive
	Lesson/Topic	My role in the meeting
Leader's Evaluation	Follow-up issues	Prayer requests

Observations during a Group Visit

Leadership Skills

Were the objectives of the meeting accomplished?

Did participants appear to be served by the meeting/leader?

Did the leader involve everyone?

Apprentice Development

What was the role of the apprentice?

What skill is the leader developing in the apprentice?

What is the next step for the apprentice?

Group Dynamics

Did the discussion flow well?

Are relationships in the group growing?

How is conflict handled?

Care

Are needs being met in this group?

Do members feel cared for?

What can this group celebrate?

How can I pray for this group?

Troubleshooting

Conflict Resolution

It is inevitable—conflict is coming soon to a group near you. Only a few groups manage to avoid conflict. Those are generally groups that are very new, groups that are not going very deep relationally, or groups that are far too polite. Conflict is a normal and natural part of group life.

So the question is, "What will you do when it comes?" Helping groups navigate conflict in a healthy manner can lead to growth for the group members, the leader, and for you as a coach. It would be helpful to review the Coaching Conversation, "Resolving Conflict in a Healthy Manner."

You may also want to review the section on conflict management in *Leading Life-Changing Small Groups* (pp. 122–26). In addition, here are some guidelines for navigating conflict:

Leaders are responsible for the process, not the outcome. You give wise counsel, guide the process, and hold people accountable. In the end, whether or not they forgive and reconcile is totally out of your hands.

The conflict need not be resolved in one meeting. Life is not a TV show—not everything can be resolved in thirty minutes. As you are dealing with the conflict, give some space. Allow people time to process their thoughts and feelings. Allow time to work things out and to heal.

Conflict must be processed with trust and confidentiality. There is great potential for additional wounding if confidentiality is not held high. Don't discuss this matter with people outside the group, unless it is truly someone from whom you are seeking wisdom and insight.

Prepare your heart. Recommend a time of prayer and solitude, often a half or whole day, for each person involved in the conflict to prepare their heart for the process they are going to walk through.

Start soon. Waiting will only deepen the wounds and prolong the pain.

Meet face-to-face. Email and telephones are great for some things, but not for conflict resolution. Letters and emails only document the offense and allow people to read into our words. So set the appointment by phone and meet face-to-face to talk.

Keep it simple. If the conflict is between two group members, then according to Matthew 18, they should talk to each other first. You may need to encourage them or hold them accountable for doing this.

Affirm the relationship. This is always the starting point when you meet. The goal is to restore a broken relationship or to help a person grow. And if you didn't love the person or value the relationship, you wouldn't be meeting—so start there.

Get the facts. Besides offering your own observations and feelings, be sure to let the other person or people speak too. As you listen, try to discern the facts. What is really going on here? Be patient, this process will take some time.

Make observations, not accusations. Be firm and direct, talking about what you have seen, heard, felt, and understood.

Promote resolution. Remember, the goal is not to win or lose. The goal is to restore the broken relationship and move forward. Sometimes that means we agree to a solution. Sometimes we simply have to agree to disagree. And sometimes, as Proverbs 19:11 says, it is to our glory to overlook an offense. Decide together what steps, if any, they need to take on the road to resolution. And then help the group members follow through.

Encourage reconciliation. Resolving the conflict is not the end of the journey. Trust may have been broken; perhaps relationships have been damaged. Though things may feel awkward for a time, work with the leader to restore the broken relationships whenever possible.

The Open Chair: How to Add Members to a Group

The "open chair" is the most effective method for connecting seekers, church attendees, and members in existing small groups.

Consider using the material entitled "Adding Members to Your Group" in *Leading Life-Changing Small Groups* (pp. 161–66) to help your leaders see the vision and understand the strategy for adding new members.

Talk often with your leaders about their relational contacts outside the small group. In what ways are they building relationships with people outside their group? Are any of these people potential new members for the group? Would group involvement be an appropriate next step spiritually for this person?

Encourage the leader to ask group members about their relational contacts as well.

Help your leaders use social events or other informal gatherings as a chance to invite prospective group members.

Pray with and for your leaders that God will bring someone to fill the empty chair in their group. Encourage the leader to spend time in prayer for the open chair at their next group meeting.

Utilize the Coaching Conversation "Becoming an Inclusive Community" (see page 99) to determine next steps the leader can take in this area.

Helping Group Leaders with Apprentice Selection and Development

Much of the material concerning apprentice development for group leaders is covered in *Leading Life-Changing Small Groups*. Topics to review with your leaders include:

- Why an apprentice leader is needed
- How to find an apprentice
- Overcoming objections
- Responsibilities of an apprentice
- How to develop an apprentice

In addition to that material, here are some guidelines to help your leaders find and develop an apprentice leader:

- Discuss their progress in this area in one-on-one meetings.
- Spend time in huddles and one-on-one meetings reviewing the material on apprenticing from *Leading Life-Changing Small Groups* or a similar resource that addresses the topic.
- Role play with the leader. Show them how you would approach a potential apprentice.
- Visit their small group to assist them in finding potential apprentices.
- Meet with leaders and apprentices together in huddles or in one-on-ones.
- Encourage potential apprentices to attend huddles and training events.
- Utilize Coaching Conversation 8, "Developing Future Leaders" (pages 80–81) to discuss the leader's progress and struggles in developing an apprentice.

Group Multiplication (Birthing)

The coach plays an important role in the vision for and birth of a small group. Leaders need to see birthing as a by-product, not the goal. When apprentices are trained and when groups fill the open chair, groups multiply. It's a natural and healthy part of the growth process. Refer to the section entitled "Birthing" in *Leading Life-Changing Small Groups* to refresh your understanding of the multiplication process.

Typically there will be apprehension about birthing from the members of the group. Remember to help everyone, including the leader, apprentice, and group members through the process. Here are a few tips for helping leaders with group multiplication:

Cast Vision. Use your huddles, visits to small groups, and one-on-one times to cast a vision for birthing. Help people understand the biblical mandate to make disciples and to connect others in community.

Provide Affirmation. When you visit a group, affirm the work that has already been done. Encourage the use of the open chair. Affirm the apprentice in his or her growth toward leadership. As groups grow, encourage them to discuss birthing and its advantages. Remind them that birthing does not mean the end of relationships, but the maturing of them.

Participate in the Process. Meet with the leader and the apprentice to discuss their birthing strategy as well as what will be communicated to the group. Help them embrace the vision for birthing and the importance of encouraging the group members through the process.

Your Role. Determine the desirability of your attending the last meeting of the small group that is about to birth. The group members and its leadership will work with you to make this decision. Often you will not need to attend, but be available if asked. Go in the role of an encourager and supporter.

Follow Up. Contact both leaders throughout the birth and see if you can be of assistance in any way. Use your huddle times to celebrate and pray for the new leaders and apprentices.

Administration. You will need to orient your new leader to their new responsibilities. Arrange a time to meet as soon as possible, even before the actual birth if you can. Begin forming a relationship and shaping a Care Covenant.

▶ Development Aid

Raising Up an Apprentice Coach

There are four steps to raising up an apprentice coach who will carry on the legacy of ministry:

1. Identify
2. Recruit
3. Develop
4. Commission

1. Identifying an Apprentice: What Do I Look For?

Not all small group leaders possess the giftedness, desire, or ability to shepherd other leaders. Remember, the position of a coach is not a promotion from being a small group leader. Rather, it is another place of service. Sometimes your best small group leaders are designed by God to be most effective and satisfied in that role.

Here are some questions that will help you identify a potential coach apprentice:

- Who is gifted and designed by God to oversee leaders?
- Who shows evidence of having the ability to develop people?
- Who has birthed (multiplied) their group and enjoys shepherding those new leaders?
- Who can be flexible enough to visit groups and arrange huddles in a way that honors the leaders?
- Who appears able to think clearly about the ministry structure and goals of the church?
- Who has a vision for the ministry of small groups at the church?

2. Recruiting an Apprentice: How Do I Approach a Potential Apprentice?

The best context to identify and recruit an apprentice coach is during your group visits and huddle times.

- Observe the level of participation and maturity of each of your leaders.
- Discuss with leaders what they are doing to develop their apprentices.
- Discuss past training or experience that would prepare them to be an apprentice coach.

How to challenge them:

- Invite a prospective apprentice to observe you leading a huddle, group visit, or one-on-one. Ask them to evaluate the meeting and its effectiveness.
- Ask the prospective apprentice to participate in planning or leading a huddle.
- Observe their ability, passion, and impact on other leaders.
- If the previous steps are positive, challenge them to consider becoming your apprentice.

▶

3. Developing an Apprentice: How Do I Equip My Apprentice for Leadership?

A skilled carpenter develops an apprentice gradually and methodically, teaching one skill at a time. Follow these basic guidelines:

- Ask your apprentice to observe you when you coach.
- Provide opportunities to ask questions or make observations.
- Gradually give them more responsibility. Visit a group together and interact with the leader before and after the meeting.
- Assist in problem-solving and conflict management.
- Encourage participation in training and small group events.
- Provide helpful feedback and encouragement to the apprentice.
- Ask them to shepherd other leaders or apprentice leaders in your huddle. These leaders can form the nucleus of their own huddle one day.

4. Commissioning an Apprentice: How and When Does My Apprentice Become an Official Coach?

According to Paul Hersey and Ken Blanchard, people who have spent years empowering leaders, the process of leadership development involves four steps.

- *Directing*: You are highly involved in providing most of the guidance. You do much teaching and modeling.
- *Coaching*: You observe the apprentice in action, providing tips, encouragement, and skill development.
- *Supporting*: You are available to provide help, but you allow the apprentice more freedom in decision-making and leadership issues.
- *Delegating*: You turn over significant leadership responsibility to the apprentice, providing freedom for them to take charge.

As you move through each of these steps, your directive behavior decreases and you give more responsibility to the apprentice. As an apprentice gains greater understanding of coaching, less direction and support is required. The time to launch will become clear as the apprentice is fully functioning in the role and leaders are thriving in her care.

▶ Development Aid ▶

Birthing Your Huddle

Birthing a huddle is similar to birthing a small group. As the number of leaders and apprentices grows, your huddle will become too large and your span of care will be pushed to the limit. It becomes essential that you birth. You may want to review the section entitled "Birthing" in *Leading Life-Changing Small Groups* to refresh your understanding of the multiplication process. Then follow these steps:

Prepare your leaders for the day you will birth. Cast vision for your apprentice to lead a huddle in order to meet the needs generated by growth and to continue their leadership development.

Begin equipping your apprentice for the day when he or she will become a coach and lead a new huddle. One way to do this is to subgroup your huddle. Allow your apprentice the opportunity to lead a time with a portion of your entire huddle. This will also help the apprentice form relationships with leaders they may one day coach.

Look for new apprentice coaches for you and your current apprentice. These candidates will typically be group leaders who exhibit strong spiritual character and have a desire to lead others.

Plan the date of your last huddle and include the new group leaders along with your new coach and apprentices. Celebrate your time together as a huddle and commission the new coach with prayer and words of encouragement.

Part Five

A Coach's World

While the expectations placed on a coach vary from church to church, one fact remains constant: the life of a coach can be as difficult as it is rewarding. Building and sustaining relationships, dealing with crises and challenges, and maintaining clear communication are all tasks demanding chunks of precious time and energy. Most coaches are highly committed volunteers with work weeks over fifty hours. So how can a coach balance the demands of work and ministry and still have time and energy for their family? A hobby? A life? The following guidelines can help coaches balance life and ministry.

Establish a Sustainable Pace

While Jesus did not live, travel or work alone, at times he chose to be alone ... These were times when he invested in the community of heaven so that his community of earth would so reflect his heavenly connection.

—Gareth Icenogle,
Biblical Foundations for Small Group Ministry

Look closely at the ministry of Jesus and you will see that his pace was never hurried or hectic. He had a balance between his larger, public ministry and time spent in more personal settings. It was not uncommon for Jesus to spend several days in a row teaching, healing, and being with the masses. Yet we also often see Jesus seeking out a quiet place to be with the Twelve (see Mark 6:32 for one example). There were even times when Jesus chose to leave the masses to be alone—times for rest, reflection, and solitude (Matt. 14:13; Mark 1:35; Luke 4:42). Jesus maintained a healthy rhythm in his ministry.

In a relational ministry like coaching, the work is never truly completed. New issues that need your attention will regularly surface. New problems will arise and will need to be resolved. Leaders will constantly need fresh vision and skills. Your work will more closely resemble a marathon than a sprint. And good marathoners know that staying in the race means establishing a sustainable pace. Here are some strategies to help you establish the right pace.

Plan Your Activities

Take a look at your personal calendar. As you look at the next month, begin by setting aside time for the following:

- Personal time with God
- Work obligations
- Time with family and friends
- Attending church services

Now, assuming there is any time left in your schedule, determine the best time for you to invest in your leaders. As a starting point, choose one coaching activity a week. For example, in a typical four- to six-week period, most coaches can be expected to:

- Visit one small group meeting
- Have a one-on-one meeting with a group leader
- Conduct a leadership gathering for their group leaders
- Meet one-on-one with their ministry leader (staff person or senior coach)
- Participate in a leadership gathering with other coaches
- Maintain regular contact with each leader through phone and email

Mark these items on your calendar as well. Now take a look at the calendar overall. Is the pace sustainable? There will always be seasons in life and ministry that are busier than others. But when those seasons stretch into months, you are risking burnout. To help avoid burnout, schedule two more items into your calendar:

1. *Margin.* Avoid the temptation to fill every waking moment with planned activity. Intentionally create open spaces in your calendar—even if you have to write them in as "margin." Creating margin allows space in your life for unplanned or unexpected events.
2. *Replenishment Time.* What is it that makes life fun for you? What gives you energy for life and ministry? When was the last time you did that activity? Set aside time to replenish yourself with a hobby, vacation, recreation, exercise, or rest.

Block off margin and replenishment times on your calendar and guard them carefully. They are keys to your health and your ability to thrive long-term in the coaching role.

Sample Stress Management Calendar

	Sunday	Monday	Tuesday	Wednesday	Thursday	Friday	Saturday
Morning	Church	Work	Work	Work	Work	Work	Soccer practice
Afternoon		Work	Work	Work	Work	Work	Yard work
Evening	Huddle		Kids' soccer game		Phone calls to leaders		Family outing

A stress management calendar is a helpful tool to evaluate the pace of your activity as a coach. After scheduling all your activities and obligations, use this calendar to check your stress load. Below are some tips to filling in the calendar:

- If you have a work, family, or ministry obligation in the time block, place an *X* in that block. Do this whether the commitment occupies only an hour or the entire time block.
- Now count the open blocks. Three or fewer empty blocks signals a very stressful pace of life.
- Work toward the goal of at least four to five open blocks in every week, and at least one day every week that has all three blocks open (margin and replenishment time).

My Stress Management Calendar

	Sunday	Monday	Tuesday	Wednesday	Thursday	Friday	Saturday
Morning							
Afternoon							
Evening							

Maximize Your Time

You have a limited amount of time to invest in coaching your leaders. For that reason, it is important to concentrate on the goals and activities that advance your ministry with them. In some seasons your leaders will be better served if you concentrate on one aspect of the coaching role, like one-on-one meetings. That extra time in individual meetings may mean that you lessen the frequency of huddles or group visits. Remember, the goal is not to hold meetings! It is to develop and nurture your leaders.

To make the most of your time, you may also want to double up on meetings or appointments. Suppose you are going to visit a group on Tuesday night. Could you save another night out by meeting with another leader before or after the visit?

Create Care Covenants

We carry expectations into every relationship. They encompass needs, desires, hopes, and dreams. Leaders and coaches each carry their own expectations into any coaching relationship. Leaders have hopes and fears of what will happen with a new coach—of how they will be cared for and developed. Coaches have a mixture of their own and the church's expectations for their relationship with a leader.

Talking through these expectations will help clearly define what will and will not happen in the relationship between coach and leader. Finding common ground and forming an agreement on these expectations is the basis of a Care Covenant. Forming a Care Covenant will help you manage your leader's expectations and determine how you will care for the leader. It will also help you develop your most faithful leaders for future growth and ministry.

The leaders covenant on the next page is a sample for you to use with your leaders. It offers some simple steps to forming a Care Covenant.

Margin is the amount allowed beyond what is needed. It is something held in reserve for contingencies or unanticipated situations. Margin is the gap between rest and exhaustion, the space between breathing freely and suffocating. It is the leeway we once had between ourselves and our limits.

—Richard Swenson, *Margin*

▶ Development Aid ▷

Care Covenant

This Care Covenant will help establish the nature of the coaching relationship you would like to have with a group leader. Each leader is unique, possessing their own blend of gifts, talents, experiences, and opportunities for growth. This tool will help you custom-tailor a relationship that will allow you to build into their spiritual life and develop their leadership skills. This guide is a helpful tool in your first face-to-face meetings with new leaders. Parts of this tool can also serve as a periodic review of your relationship.

Explore Their Story

1. Ask the leader to share his/her spiritual journey. How did they come into a relationship with Christ?
2. How did the person come to be a part of this church?
3. How did they come into group leadership?

Discuss Expectations

1. Ask the leader to think through what care and support they would like to receive from you as a coach. It may help to think through any previous coaching relationships and determine what was helpful and what was not.
2. Think about your expectations for the relationship with this leader.
3. Meet face-to-face to talk through these desires and expectations.
4. Come to a consensus on what can and cannot be expected from each person in this relationship.

Agree on Values to Affirm

Transparency: We will share our feelings, struggles, joys, and hurts with each other, with candor and mutual acceptance.

Honesty: We will be honest with each other by speaking the truth in love.

Safety: We will respect each other's opinions, as well as allowing for differences of opinion in a spirit of mutual love.

Confidentiality: Anything personal shared in confidentiality stays between the two of us unless permission is given.

Priority: We will make our meetings a priority, and if either of us is unable to attend or is running late, we will call ahead.

Other Values:

Maintain Clear Communication

Communication is the lifeblood of your ministry. Clear communication keeps the purpose, plans, and vision of the ministry in focus for you, your leaders, and the group members. So as you interact with ministry staff, other coaches, and group leaders, ask yourself, "What information do I need to share that will help them in their role?" Think in terms of:

Group Leaders: What do I need to communicate or clarify regarding the vision? About upcoming events or activities? Church-wide plans or initiatives?

Coaches: What am I currently working through with my leaders that would benefit other coaches in the church? What struggles and successes can I share? What new things am I learning?

Ministry Staff: You are on the front lines of the small groups ministry. You know the challenges and needs of your leaders and their group members. You know the stories of life-change. Consistent, clear communication with ministry staff will encourage them when the vision is becoming reality. It will also point out areas where improvement or additional training may be necessary.

You can communicate with ministry staff through a variety of means—in person, over the phone, through voicemail, or email. Remember to choose the medium that is most appropriate for the information you are communicating. Some news and general information can be communicated through email, and doing so saves valuable meeting time for more delicate or difficult issues.

Live in Community

Coaches need community for the same reasons as everyone else. You need a place to be known and loved, a place for taking faith risks, and a place where you can be challenged to develop spiritually.

If we desire to remain and grow in Christ, we need community. Yet finding a small group where it is safe to be real and vulnerable can be a challenge for coaches. When a coach walks into a group, a certain level of skill and wisdom is assumed by group members and leaders. It can be difficult to take off the coach hat and put on a group member hat.

So where and how can coaches find community? Some experience community as they meet with their leaders or fellow coaches. Others find a type of community as they meet one-on-one with their leaders. While both of these experiences are good, they will not fully meet a coach's need for community.

Here are two possible solutions:

1. *Join an existing small group*. Establish clear boundaries and expectations with the leader and the group. Be clear that you are attending simply as a member, not a coach. You are there to participate, not to evaluate or guide.

2. *Coaches community*. You may want to consider forming a small group with other coaches. Be careful that this is really community and not just a business meeting.

Know When to Step Down

To be a coach is to serve in a high-impact role in the church. The sky is the limit on making a difference, but the pressures and demands can be intense as well. Problems rarely surface at a convenient time, people can be messy, conflict resolution is seldom neat and tidy, and the list goes on and on.

Even when coaches do their best to establish and maintain a healthy rhythm, things change. Life circumstances can impact your coaching. Personal illness or struggles, family challenges, like aging parents or special needs in your children, changes in or the loss of employment—all have an impact on your capacity for ministry.

Because of the close relationship that often develops between coaches and their leaders, making the decision to step down can be very difficult. The close ties can cloud your judgment, and knowing when to quit can be tough.

Some coaches want to wave the white flag of surrender too soon. When their first small group experiences conflict or trouble, or when a leader doesn't respond immediately to their leadership, they take these difficulties as an indicator that they are a failure as a coach and should step down.

But there are others who more closely resemble first-century martyrs. In spite of personal struggle and loss, they refuse to quit. They are determined to persevere—to quit would be viewed as personal failure. The truth is these coaches often hang on too long, to the detriment of their leaders and to their own soul.

So how do you know when the load is too heavy? How do you know when you need to take a break from coaching? Here are some questions to help you think through this tough issue. Do a quick checkup and put a check mark beside the statements that are true for you:

- ☐ It has been more than three weeks since I have had any contact with my leaders.
- ☐ When I think about how I am doing as a coach, I feel shame or guilt.
- ☐ I continually feel that ministry demands are overwhelming.
- ☐ I feel resentment when the church staff or leaders ask for assistance.
- ☐ I find myself having strong reactions to ministry difficulties.
- ☐ I struggle to fully engage my heart in worship.
- ☐ My desire to practice spiritual disciplines is decreasing.
- ☐ I constantly feel hurried, wishing for one more hour or day to get things done.
- ☐ Intense emotions, anger, or tears seem to be constantly near the surface.

While this list is not exhaustive, checking off more than two items ought to cause you some concern. Either the ministry demands are too great (whether

It is the responsibility of every Christian to carve out a satisfying life under the rule of God—so that sin won't look so good.
—Dallas Willard

imposed by yourself or others) or your capacity has diminished. Did you check four or more? You're in the danger zone.

A conversation with a staff member or senior coach would be a good start to figuring out why you feel this pressure and what can be done to resolve it. You may be expecting too much of yourself. You may have misunderstood the church's expectations of coaches. Perhaps you have signed up to volunteer in other ministries in the church and the combined expectations are overwhelming. Or you may be in a season of life where the demands of coaching are too much for you.

Whatever the reason, do yourself and your leaders a favor. Sit down with a staff member or ministry leader and talk through this. Spend time alone with God in prayer, seeking his heart for you. Seek out godly counsel to help determine if you should take a break from coaching.

Part Six

Building a Coaching Structure

This material is designed to help those who are:

1. *The Small Group Point Person.* In other words, you are responsible for building the small group ministry in a local church. This guide will help you address the issues related specifically to building a coaching structure. To meet other challenges in building this ministry (like connecting people to groups, designing a leadership development strategy, and helping your senior leaders articulate the small group vision to the congregation) we suggest you read *The Seven Deadly Sins of Small Group Ministry: A Troubleshooting Guide for Church Leaders.* It will help you identify, assess, and address seven major areas that every small group ministry struggles with in order to thrive. This work will help you diagnose problems and recommend workable solutions.

2. *Senior Coaches.* Senior coaches are seasoned coaches who are now shepherding other coaches and helping the church build the small group ministry. Or perhaps one day you may be asked (or called) to lead the small group ministry in your church.

3. *Elders, Deacons, and Board Members.* You have probably given the pastoral staff authority and direction for moving ahead with developing a small group ministry. This material will give you insight into the key issues related to church structure as the ministry grows and matures.

Finally, if you are responsible for building the small group ministry in a local church and are just beginning that process, it would be helpful to read *Building a Church of Small Groups,* also by Bill Donahue and Russ Robinson. This material is foundational for communicating a theology of community, understanding the essentials of small group relationships, getting your first group of leaders started, and making the strategic decisions necessary for expanding the ministry throughout the church.

A Guide for Small Group Ministry Point Leaders

We have often said that, humanly speaking, the most strategic person in the life-change process is the small group leader. It is the leader who has life-to-life contact with people, and in a church that relies heavily on small groups, leaders are on the "front lines" of ministry. However, small group leaders are not the only strategic people.

When it comes to the entire life-change structure, the small group coach is indispensable. Their role in supporting leaders is crucial to the ongoing success and growth of the small group ministry. Once you get a group of leaders started, they will need some coaching and support. Without coaches, the support system for leaders, the small group leader becomes isolated and feels stranded on some ministry island far from the mainland of the local church. Yet developing and retaining coaches continues to be one of the most challenging tasks for small group ministry point leaders.

This material is divided into eight steps that offer guidelines to help you design, build, and maintain a workable coaching structure.

1. Clearly Define the Coaching Role

Role clarity is essential for every coach. In this resource we have described the four key coaching practices in detail so your coaches know what they are to do. To review this material, look again at part 3 of this book.

Take time to meet with existing or potential coaches and review this framework. Help them understand what each of these four key practices means and what the ministry expectations are for each of them.

- Model
- Guide
- Envision
- Equip

If you have a different coaching framework or use different phrases to communicate the "job description" or "ministry profile" for a coach, that's fine. The key is to be clear and make sure coaches understand exactly what is expected.

2. Recruiting Coaches

Recruiting coaches is difficult because most people imagine they must be a small group expert or a seasoned and wise mentor when they hear the word "coach." Most envision a hard-driving football coach or a sage with years of experience helping people grow spiritually. The thought of coaching can appear overwhelming, so be sure to communicate that a coach is a supportive, prayerful, relational person who is interested in getting alongside small group leaders to help *them* be successful. Explain that a coach is not "Big Brother" (or sister!) snooping around, looking for problems. A coach is not a demanding boss like some people might have at work. Rather, use the image of a golf or tennis coach, someone who provides feedback and insight, connecting leaders to resources that will help their small groups flourish.

Recruiting Strategies

1. *Sharing ministry together.* Give prospective coaches one leader to encourage and watch the potential coach grow (use the Peer Coaching Model described in number 8 below). If they do this well, encourage prospective coaches to take on one to two more leaders and move toward coaching.

2. *Include prospective coaches in leadership gatherings.* When you bring leaders together for dinners, retreats, or training sessions, you have an opportunity to expose prospective coaches to others who are in the role already. They can ask questions and hear stories of life-change.

3. *Take prospective coaches on visits to small groups.* When you visit a group to provide encouragement and support to a leader, take a prospective coach along. Debrief what took place later over a cup of coffee and help them see that such visits are one aspect of coaching. As it is frequently said, "Ministry is caught more than taught." You may have to model this for them.

Generally speaking, allow leaders to grow into coaching—don't simply make them *go* into coaching, unprepared for what lies ahead.

What to Look For

Look for people with previous small group leadership experience who:

- Love Christ and the church
- Take an interest in other leaders
- Get excited about the overall ministry of the church
- Have a passion for helping others become successful
- Are willing to take a risk
- Trust you and your judgment
- Are teachable and open to learning new ways of doing ministry
- Are effective (not perfect) small group leaders

Remember that the most effective leaders may want to remain as small group leaders—because God made them for that role! An effective coach is one with good group experience but is gifted to influence others through a ministry of reproduction. A leader who needs a weekly meeting and enjoys lots of personal discipleship may not make a good coach, unless they also enjoy discipling leaders. The coach's ministry is to a leadership audience primarily, and the sphere of influence is different than that of a small group leader.

3. Choose and Establish a Structure

Structures are not glamorous. If well designed, however, they free both group leaders and coaches to accomplish the ministry. The structure shown on the next page allows a coach to invest time and energy into leaders, especially new

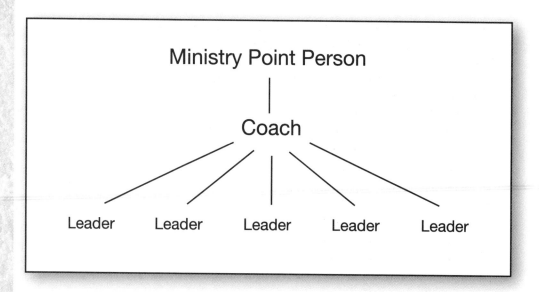

leaders who need direction and a listening, prayerful person to empower them. The 1:5 ratio defines the maximum "span of care" that a coach should have as a volunteer. In this model, a coach would care for up to five leaders.

In this model, each leader feels cared for, has access to a coach, and has a peer relationship to other leaders. This forms a "leadership community" that can be fostered and developed over time. This initial structure can be modified as coaches and group leaders become more experienced. Other models are discussed later in this section.

4. The Transition from Group Leader to Coach

Moving a small group leader from leader to coach is a process, one that can be gradual (as mentioned above) or more sudden. The process depends on the kind of leader you are working with. Leading a group while coaching other leaders creates a demanding span of care. If a coach has eight to ten group members and is coaching two to three leaders, the result can be overwhelming, a span of care of thirteen people. This can be a strain unless the coach is semi-retired or can reasonably invest greater than average time in the ministry. Once a coach is shepherding more than two leaders, it is suggested that they focus primarily on coaching. Encourage them to remain a member of a small group if they wish, and even help share the leadership if that is not a burden. But being both a coach and a small group leader can be a challenge the average busy person cannot handle.

5. Skill Development for Coaches

Coaches need some basic skills to fulfill their ministry. Parts 3 and 4 of this manual contain the skill sets you will need to train your coaches. In addition to these skills, here are a few training tips.

Keep training clear and specific. Once coaches have completed an initial training workshop or orientation, keep training experiences focused on one or two skills at a time. Try to deliver the entire session in thirty minutes, and certainly less than an hour.

Design training that fits the schedule of the coach. Coaches have full lives and already make schedule adjustments to meet leaders and visit groups. Try to have training gatherings (huddles, workshops) at times when they are already coming to the church building. Or take training to a group of coaches in a home at a time convenient for them. We have found that tagging it on to an existing event or service is easiest, and child care and other resources are usually available at these times. During the adult Sunday school hour is also a good time.

Do not use training time to simply communicate information. Use email, a website, or a newsletter to communicate information about events, special dates, church issues, and so on. Don't waste the training time. Quickly give people an update and direct them to the resource (newsletter, bulletin, etc.) for more information. Spend your time investing in them as leaders.

Include biblical teaching. Every time you gather, speak truth from Scripture to encourage, edify, or challenge coaches. Remind them why their job is so essential. Read passages about relationships, shepherding, ministry, prayer, and leadership. God's Word renews and refreshes leaders at every phase of development, and coaches need this as much as anyone.

Make it creative and interesting. Don't just teach—train! Training utilizes interaction and practicing skills and conversations with other leaders and coaches. Consider using case studies of actual small group situations. Promote dialogue and mutual problem solving. Use appropriate DVD or video clips to inspire or to create some humor. Spend time in prayer around tables or in a circle. Model small group life. Mix up the order each time, and always include some kind of food or snacks!

Provide take-away tools, handouts, or resources. Never let coaches leave empty-handed. Give them a copy of a great message to listen to or a sheet filled with tips and ideas for leading a huddle meeting with their small group leaders. (We included some in this resource. After using these, you can develop some of your own.) Give them materials they can hand out to their small group leaders, such as lists of icebreaker questions, discussion ideas, and creative ways to use the Bible in a group. Or give them an interesting article to read to encourage them.

Get immediate feedback. Ask how the training session went. Was it too long? Did it hit the mark? What would improve it? What issues are coaches facing that need addressing right away or the next time you gather? Do they need more time in prayer or for problem solving? What is the best format for training? As you ask these questions, you will get valuable information to improve your next training session and your communication tools.

6. The Care and Nurture of Coaches

Treat coaches as you want them to treat leaders. Spend time with them in smaller groups. Getting them together at your home with their families, meeting them for lunches, and breakfast meetings are all ways to show a personal interest in them and their ministry. Here are some tips.

- Focus on coaches as people first, not as the "ministry."
- Emphasize nurture, not development.
- Make the goal be for them to feel loved and cared for and to have a safe place to talk.
- Link them to "peer" coaches with whom they can share needs, ideas, and feelings about the ministry.

- Pray and read Scripture with them.
- Ask how you can serve them.
- Express interest in things that interest them—birthdays, children's events, or hobbies.
- Make certain that you or other staff are responsible for initiating contact with coaches. Don't wait for them to call with a problem.

7. Factors That Help the Longevity of Coaches

Coaches will stick around if you stick with them, building into them. Coaches and leaders rarely leave a ministry to which they feel called and in which they develop deep, lasting relationships with God and others. Your job as the point person, overseeing the small group ministry, is to create an environment for spiritual growth and support, as well as personal care and ministry resources. Consider the following:

- Give coaches resources, like great books or CDs/tapes to encourage their growth and to inspire them.
- Provide an annual retreat just for them.
- Consider a quarterly lunch after a church service to give them ministry updates.
- Include them in ministry planning, giving them ownership of the ministry.
- Appropriately recognize them for their contribution.
- Step in and provide support for their leaders when the coach is in a particularly taxing season of life (death of a family member, loss of job, health challenge).
- Invest in them spiritually at a retreat that focuses on prayer and Scripture, or do this quarterly for an evening or on a Saturday morning, whichever works for your coaches.
- Remember, the structure exists to serve the leaders—the leaders do not exist to serve your structure. Change the structure when it is not working.
- Spend time listening! Get information from coaches and use it to make decisions about the direction and focus of the ministry.

Coaches will enjoy spending time with you, because you have both a personal and a developmental interest in them.

8. Alternative Coaching Models

Coaching structures will vary based on your small group ministry model or your church structure. One fundamental issue that determines a strategy is the span of care you want a coach or staff person to have. How many leaders do you want each coach to provide care for? Also, how much do you want a coach to do? If you simply want coaches to provide communication and ministry updates, and no real development of leaders, coaches can connect with more leaders in their ministry on a regular basis. However, if you want coaches to invest personally in leaders, meet and pray with them, and visit them in their ministry context (a small group meeting) to better understand the challenges and opportunities they face, then the span of care will have to be smaller.

Developmental Model: 1:5 Ratio. Here the coach can Guide, Model, Envision, and Equip leaders because the span is small and the ministry is focused. Each leader gets a lot of attention and care, can be fully known and loved, and can be developed according to gifts and leadership potential. This model is the primary approach advocated in this book for churches just beginning a small group ministry or those that are now adding coaches to that ministry.

Peer Coaching Model: One-to-One Mentoring. This model allows someone to begin coaching while still leading a group. It means that a more experienced leader can bring support to a newer leader. This model does not require much structure.

Mass Coaching Model: 1:25 Ratio. Some churches use this to communicate to a large number of leaders. The focus is communication, information, and group gatherings for training. Individual coaching is harder to accomplish because of the sheer numbers involved (1:25). Churches using this model usually pay a part-time coach to work about ten hours a week.

Hands-Free Model: No Specific Coach. Churches use this with very experienced leaders. They require little coaching and development, so these leaders are usually "coached" through email, events, broader leadership gatherings, and occasional contact with church staff.

Senior Coaching Model: Developmental 1:5 Model Expanded. When a coach is very experienced in coaching leaders, they can begin to shepherd and develop less experienced coaches. A senior coach may have three to five coaches who each shepherd three to five leaders. This is a volunteer position, yet it allows a qualified coach the opportunity to influence multiple leaders and coaches. Typically it is used in larger churches with more than fifty groups.

Your responsibility as a point leader is to use a workable model. We suggest you begin with a basic 1:5 ratio and build from there. As your structure grows and your leaders develop, you can add variations. But stick with the basics first, building a developmental mindset into your people. Yes, you can coach larger numbers of leaders, but make sure you are providing development, not simply information. Distinguish between a communication model and a development model. It all boils down to what you want a coach to do.

Conclusion

We've compiled this book to provide you with a variety of tools and ministry aids for shepherding small group leaders. Our hope is that you will be able to employ this as a reference guide, using what you need when you need it.

The small group movement is growing worldwide, and the need for leadership grows with it. Thank you for taking on this role. As people who have coached many leaders, we understand your initial apprehension and fears. We also understand the rewards of seeing ministry multiplied into dozens of lives because of an investment in a few leaders. That's the privilege of coaching.

When small group leaders Wes and Stephanie came home from the hospital with baby Eli on October 6, 2004, they had high hopes for a full and exciting life with their newborn son. But tragically, just one week later, he fell asleep and simply did not wake up. From the shock and sadness of the emergency room where revival efforts failed, the distraught couple called their coaches. The couple explained,

> Before we left the hospital that evening our coaches were with us and did not leave our sides. They handled all the practical matters, like picking up pizza and going to the grocery store. Then, the next day they came to the funeral home to help make preparations for the ceremony, making phone calls and organizing the service in just two days. The chapel was packed as several hundred people attended.

> We were amazed, and we are still amazed. I do not know where we'd be without our small group and our coaches. I am sure the next several months will be filled with the ups and downs of grief, but it is a great comfort to know that we will not be going through it alone. We have our friends and family at Willow Creek to walk with us through our valley.

Imagine the great satisfaction these coaches had in helping the leaders—who had become part of their spiritual families—through the toughest days of life. They had the privilege of developing these leaders, but now they had become their friends in time of need.

These leaders did not need a boss or a manager at this critical time in life; they needed friends. They needed someone who knew them and who would walk with them not just through the funeral but through the days of joy and grief to follow. Someone who takes a deep interest in their ministry, spiritual growth, and family—a loving shepherd who has their best interests in mind.

That's what leaders need. And that is what you can be for them. And your church is going to experience a greater level of community and care than ever before, because of coaches and leaders who are willing to shepherd the body of Christ together.

We pray that God will bless your efforts as you coach leaders and build a coaching structure that helps you shepherd the people in your congregation. It is our privilege to help you and cheer you on. Feel free to contact us at *www.willowcreek.com* if we can serve you in any way.

—*Bill Donahue and Greg Bowman*

Building a Church of Small Groups

A Place Where Nobody Stands Alone

Bill Donahue and Russ Robinson

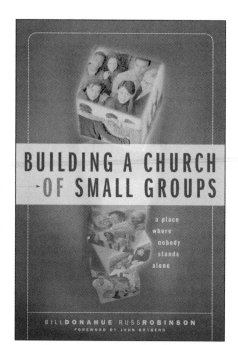

Our hearts were made for community. We hunger for the deep, authentic relationships Jesus had in mind when he prayed that his followers would be one. Yet in many churches, the connection we crave is lacking. How can church become a place where nobody stands alone?

Through small groups. Like nothing else, they provide the kind of life-giving community that builds and empowers the body of Christ and impacts the world. At Willow Creek Community Church, small groups are so important that they define the core organizational strategy. Bill Donahue and Russ Robinson write, "We have gone from a church with small groups … to being a church of small groups."

Donahue and Robinson share revealing glimpses of Willow Creek's journey to becoming a church where over 18,000 people connect in 2,700 small groups. And they tell how your church—whatever its size and circumstances—can become a place where men and women, adults and children, can experience powerful, transforming community.

Building a Church of Small Groups unpacks the vision, values, and strategies required to integrate small groups into your entire ministry. Part 1 presents the theological, sociological, and organizational underpinnings of small groups. You'll discover why small groups, as reflections of God's communal nature, are so vital to church health.

Part 2 moves you from vision to practice. Here is how to develop thriving small groups based on authentic relationships, where truth and life intersect, conflict leads to growth, and skilled leaders help group members mature into fully devoted followers of Christ.

Part 3 shows you how to identify, recruit, and train group leaders and provide them with long-term coaching and support. Finally, in part 4, you'll learn how to deal with the critical process of change as your church develops its small group ministry.

Written by two of today's top authorities on small group ministry, *Building a Church of Small Groups* is a proven blueprint for health and spiritual vitality in your church. Here is thorough, seasoned guidance for helping people grow together in faith, heart, and lives through closely knit small group communities.

Softcover: 0-310-26710-2

Pick up a copy today at your favorite bookstore!

ZONDERVAN™

GRAND RAPIDS, MICHIGAN 49530 USA

WWW.ZONDERVAN.COM

WILLOW
Willow Creek Resources

Walking the
Small Group Tightrope

Meeting the Challenges Every Group Faces

Bill Donahue and Russ Robinson

Six Ways to Improve Your Balance as a Group Leader

Leading a successful small group is like walking a tightrope. You traverse a taut, exciting line, balancing the dynamic tensions characteristic of every group. Drawing on the concept of "polarity management," Bill Donahue and Russ Robinson help you understand and deal with six dynamic areas every group leader must manage in order to create genuine, transforming small group community.

Your group is in for unprecedented connection and growth when you harness the interplay between

- Truth and Life
- Care and Discipleship
- Friendship and Accountability
- Kindness and Confrontation
- Task and People
- Openness and Intimacy

Effective, life-giving small groups learn how to embrace both ends of each continuum. *Walking the Small Group Tightrope* will strengthen your sense of balance, help you gain confidence as a leader, and show you how to release the untapped creative and relational energy in your group.

Softcover: 0-310-25229-6

Pick up a copy today at your favorite bookstore!

Leading Life-Changing Small Groups

Bill Donahue and the Willow Creek Small Groups Team

The bestselling small group guidebook— over 100,000 sold. NOW UPDATED.

Like nothing else, small groups have the power to change lives. They're the ideal route to discipleship—a place where the rubber of biblical truth meets the road of human relationships.

For six years Bill Donahue provided training and resources for small group leaders so that Willow Creek could build a church of small groups. Now he is committed to creating tools that will help church leaders pursue the same goal—to provide a place in community for everyone in their congregation. In *Leading Life-Changing Small Groups*, Donahue and his team share in depth the practical insights that have made Willow Creek's small group ministry so effective.

The Comprehensive, Ready-Reference Guide for Small Group Leaders

The unique, ready-reference format of this book gives small group leaders, pastors, church leaders, educators, and counselors a commanding grasp of:

- Group formation and values
- Leadership requirements and responsibilities
- The philosophy and structure of small groups
- Meeting preparation and participation
- Discipleship within the group
- Leadership training ... and much more

From an individual group to an entire small group ministry, *Leading Life-Changing Small Groups* gives you the comprehensive guidance you need to cultivate life-changing small groups ... and growing, fruitful followers of Christ.

Softcover: 0-310-24750-0

Pick up a copy today at your favorite bookstore!

ZONDERVAN™

GRAND RAPIDS, MICHIGAN 49530 USA

WWW.ZONDERVAN.COM

WILLOW

Willow Creek Resources

Seven Deadly Sins of Small Group Ministry

A Troubleshooting Guide for Church Leaders

Bill Donahue and Russ Robinson

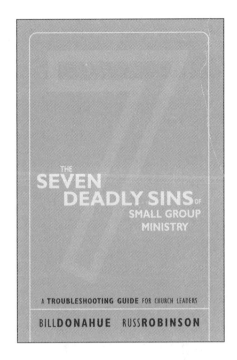

It's one thing to start a small group ministry. It's another to keep the groups in your church healthy and headed in the same direction. Whatever your church's approach may be—whether it is a church with groups or of groups—sooner or later, as a leader, you'll need to do some troubleshooting. That's when the expert, to-the-point guidance in this book will prove its worth.

In *The Seven Deadly Sins of Small Group Ministry*, what would take you years to learn through trial and error is distilled into some of the most useful information you can find. Drawing on the knowledge they've gleaned from working inside Willow Creek Community Church, from consulting with hundreds of churches, and from conducting conferences and seminars worldwide, small group experts Bill Donahue and Russ Robinson furnish you with proven, real-life solutions to the knottiest problems in your small group ministry. This is no theory—it's hands-on stuff you can read and apply today.

The beauty of this book lies in its unique diagnostic process. It allows you to assess, diagnose, and correct seven common "deadly sins" that can drain the life from your church's small group ministry. Here are the strategies and tools you need to deal with

1. Unclear Ministry Objectives
2. Lack of Point Leadership
3. Poor Coaching Structures
4. Neglect of Ongoing Leadership Development
5. Closed Group Mind-set
6. Narrow Definition of a Small Group
7. Neglect of Assimilation Process

The Seven Deadly Sins of Small Group Ministry is indispensable for every small group director, church staff, ministry leader, and senior pastor. It's strong medicine for the ailments that threaten the small groups in your church.

Softcover: 0-310-26711-0

Pick up a copy today at your favorite bookstore!

ZONDERVAN™

GRAND RAPIDS, MICHIGAN 49530 USA

WWW.ZONDERVAN.COM

WILLOW

Willow Creek Resources

Pursuing Spiritual Transformation
Bible Study Series Sampler

John Ortberg, Laurie Pederson, and Judson Poling

This series from Willow Creek is designed to motivate and guide believers in an exciting process of personal change. The first study, *Fully Devoted*, introduces participants to the core ideas behind transformation, and each of the remaining five guides covers one of the five "G's": Gifts, Giving, Grace, Groups, and Growth in seven sessions each.

Combo Pack: 0-310-64277-9

Pick up a copy today at your favorite bookstore!

GRAND RAPIDS, MICHIGAN 49530 USA

WWW.ZONDERVAN.COM

WILLOW
Willow Creek Resources

Tough Questions Bible Study Series

Garry Poole and Judson Poling

This revised edition of Tough Questions, designed for use in any small group setting, is ideal for use in seeker small groups. Based on more than five years of field-tested feedback, extensive improvements make this bestselling series easier to use and more appealing than ever for both participants and group leaders.

The Tough Questions Series

How can an all-powerful God allow suffering? Is Jesus really the only way to God? Why should I trust the Bible?

Tough questions. Reasonable questions. The kinds of challenging questions you or someone you know may be asking that are worth taking time to explore.

In six sessions designed to get small groups thinking and interacting, each guide in the Tough Questions series deals frankly with objections commonly raised about Christianity. You'll engage in the kind of spirited dialog that shows the Christian faith can stand up to scrutiny.

Do Science and the Bible Conflict? Softcover, 0-310-24507-9
Don't All Religions Lead to God? Softcover, 0-310-24506-0
How Could God Allow Suffering and Evil? Softcover, 0-310-24505-2
How Does Anyone Know God Exists? Softcover, 0-310-24502-8
How Reliable Is the Bible? Softcover, 0-310-24504-4
What Difference Does Jesus Make? Softcover, 0-310-24503-6
Why Become a Christian? Softcover, 0-310-24508-7

Pick up a copy today at your favorite bookstore!

ZONDERVAN™

GRAND RAPIDS, MICHIGAN 49530 USA

WWW.ZONDERVAN.COM

WILLOW
Willow Creek Resources

Willow Creek Association
Vision, Training, Resources for Prevailing Churches

This resource was created to serve you and to help you build a local church that prevails. It is just one of many ministry tools that are part of the Willow Creek Resources® line, published by the Willow Creek Association together with Zondervan.

The Willow Creek Association (WCA) was created in 1992 to serve a rapidly growing number of churches from across the denominational spectrum that are committed to helping unchurched people become fully devoted followers of Christ. Membership in the WCA now numbers over 10,000 Member Churches worldwide from more than ninety denominations.

The Willow Creek Association links like-minded Christian leaders with each other and with strategic vision, training, and resources in order to help them build prevailing churches designed to reach their redemptive potential. Here are some of the ways the WCA does that.

- **Prevailing Church Conference**—an annual two-and-a-half day event, held at Willow Creek Community Church in South Barrington, Illinois, to help pioneering church leaders raise up a volunteer core while discovering new and innovative ways to build prevailing churches that reach unchurched people.

- **Leadership Summit**—a once-a-year, two-and-a-half-day conference to envision and equip Christians with leadership gifts and responsibilities. Presented live at Willow Creek as well as via satellite broadcast to over sixty locations across North America, this event is designed to increase the leadership effectiveness of pastors, ministry staff, volunteer church leaders, and Christians in the marketplace.

- **Ministry-Specific Conferences**—throughout each year the WCA hosts a variety of conferences and training events—both at Willow Creek's main campus and off-site, across the U.S. and around the world—targeting church leaders in ministry-specific areas such as: evangelism, the arts, children, students, small groups, preaching and teaching, spiritual formation, spiritual gifts, raising up resources, etc.

- **Willow Creek Resources®**—to provide churches with trusted and field-tested ministry resources in such areas as leadership, evangelism, spiritual formation, spiritual gifts, small groups, stewardship, student ministry, children's ministry, the use of the arts—drama, media, contemporary music—and more. For additional information about Willow Creek Resources® call the Customer Service Center at 800-570-9812. Outside the U.S. call 847-765-0070.

- *WillowNet*—the WCA's Internet resource service, which provides access to hundreds of transcripts of Willow Creek messages, drama scripts, songs, videos, and multimedia tools. The system allows users to sort through these elements and download them for a fee. Visit us online at www.willowcreek.com.

- *WCA News*—a quarterly publication to inform you of the latest trends, resources, and information on WCA events from around the world.

- *Defining Moments*—a monthly audio journal for church leaders featuring Bill Hybels and other Christian leaders discussing probing issues to help you discover biblical principles and transferable strategies to maximize your church's redemptive potential.

- *The Exchange*—our online classified ads service to assist churches in recruiting key staff for ministry positions.

- **Member Benefits**—includes substantial discounts to WCA training events, a 20 percent discount on all Willow Creek Resources®, access to a Members-Only section on WillowNet, monthly communications, and more. Member Churches also receive special discounts and premier services through WCA's growing number of ministry partners—Select Service Providers.

For specific information about WCA membership, upcoming conferences, and other ministry services contact:

Willow Creek Association
P.O. Box 3188, Barrington, IL 60011-3188
Phone: 847-570-9812
Fax: 847-765-5046
www.willowcreek.com

We want to hear from you. Please send your comments about this book to us in care of zreview@zondervan.com. Thank you.

ZONDERVAN™

GRAND RAPIDS, MICHIGAN 49530 USA

ZONDERVAN.COM/
AUTHOR**TRACKER**